SEXUAL VIOLENCE ON CAMPUS

Great Debates in Higher Education is a series of short, accessible books addressing key challenges to and issues in Higher Education, on a national and international level. These books are research informed but debate driven. They are intended to be relevant to a broad spectrum of researchers, students and administrators in higher education, and are designed to help us unpick and assess the state of higher education systems, policies and social and economic impacts

RECENTLY PUBLISHED IN THIS SERIES

Teaching Excellence in Higher Education: Challenges, Changes and the Teaching Excellence Framework

Amanda French and Matt O'Leary

British Universities in the Brexit Moment: Political, Economic and Cultural Implications

Mike Finn

Higher Education Funding and Access in International Perspective

Sheila Riddell, Sarah Minty, Elisabet Weedon and Susan Whittaker

Sexual Violence on Campus: Power-Conscious Approaches to Awareness, Prevention, and Response

Chris Linder

Evaluating Scholarship and Research Impact: History, Practices, and Policy Development

Jeffrey W. Alstete, Nicholas J. Beutell and John P. Meyer

Access to Success and Social Mobility Through Higher Education: A Curate's Egg?

Stuart Billingham

The Marketisation of English Higher Education: A Policy Analysis of a Risk-Based System

Colin McCaig

Refugees in Higher Education: Debate, Discourse and Practice

Jacqueline Stevenson and Sally Baker

Radicalisation and Counter-Radicalisation in Higher Education

Catherine McGlynn and Shaun McDaid

Perspectives on Access to Higher Education

Sam Broadhead, Rosemarie Davis and Anthony Hudson

Cultural Journeys in Higher Education: Student Voices and Narratives

Jan Bamford and Lucy Pollard

Degendering Leadership in Higher Education

Barret Katuna

A Brief History of Credit in UK Higher Education: Laying Siege to the Ivory Tower

Wayne Turnbull

The Fully Functioning University

Tom Bourner, Asher Rospigliosi and Linda Heath

Leadership of Historically Black Colleges and Universities: A What Not To Do Guide for HBCU Leaders

Johnny D. Jones

Challenging the Teaching Excellence Framework: Diversity Deficits in Higher Education Evaluations

Amanda French and Kate Carruthers Thomas

Combatting Marginalisation by Co-Creating Education: Methods, Theories and Practices From the Perspectives of Young People

David Thore Gravesen, Kaz Stuart, Mette Bunting, Sidse Hølvig Mikkelsen and Peter Hornbæk Frostholm

Higher Education at the Crossroads of Disruption: The University of the 21st Century

Andreas Kaplan

Reimagining Historically Black Colleges and Universities: Survival Beyond 2021

Gary B. Crosby, Khalid A. White, Marcus A. Chanay and Adriel A. Hilton

Degrees of Success: The Transitions From Vocational to Higher Education

Geoff Hayward, Eugenia Katartzi, Hubert Ertl and Michael Hoelscher

Transformational University Leadership: A Case Study for 21st Century Leaders and Aspirational Research Universities

Hilary Coulson, Yali Zou and Frank Fernandez

Theory of Change: Debates and Applications to Access and Participation in Higher Education

Samuel Dent, Anna Mountford-Zimdars and Ciaran Burke

Selling Our Youth: Graduate Stories of Class, Gender and Work in Challenging Times

Harriet Bradley, Richard Waller and Laura Bentley

From Access to Engagement and Beyond

Stuart Billingham

The Affective Researcher

Andrew G. Gibson

Arts and Academia

Carola Boehm

Recognizing Promise: The Role of Community Colleges in a Post Pandemic World

Michael A. Baston, Beatrice L. Bridglall and Michael Nettles

Building a Better Normal: Visions of Schools of Education in a Post-Pandemic World

Priya Goel, Jonathan Simmons, Smridhi Marwah, Lars Andersson, Sinikka Neuhaus and Marian Mahat

Refugees in Higher Education: Debate, Discourse and Practice (2nd edition)

Jacqueline Stevenson and Sally Baker

SEXUAL VIOLENCE ON CAMPUS

Power-Conscious Approaches to Awareness, Prevention, and Response (2nd Edition)

BY

CHRIS LINDER
University of Utah, USA

United Kingdom – North America – Japan – India
Malaysia – China

Emerald Publishing Limited
Emerald Publishing, Floor 5, Northspring, 21-23 Wellington Street,
Leeds LS1 4DL

Second edition 2025

Copyright © 2025 Chris Linder.
Published under exclusive licence by Emerald Publishing Limited.

Reprints and permissions service
Contact: www.copyright.com

No part of this book may be reproduced, stored in a retrieval system, transmitted in any form or by any means electronic, mechanical, photocopying, recording or otherwise without either the prior written permission of the publisher or a licence permitting restricted copying issued in the UK by The Copyright Licensing Agency and in the USA by The Copyright Clearance Center. Any opinions expressed in the chapters are those of the authors. Whilst Emerald makes every effort to ensure the quality and accuracy of its content, Emerald makes no representation implied or otherwise, as to the chapters' suitability and application and disclaims any warranties, express or implied, to their use.

British Library Cataloguing in Publication Data
A catalogue record for this book is available from the British Library

ISBN: 978-1-83549-116-4 (Print)
ISBN: 978-1-83549-113-3 (Online)
ISBN: 978-1-83549-115-7 (Epub)

Printed and bound by CPI Group (UK) Ltd, Croydon, CR0 4YY

INVESTOR IN PEOPLE

CONTENTS

About the Author   xi
Foreword   xiii
Preface to First Edition   xix
Acknowledgments   xxv
Introduction   xxix

1. Developing a Power-Conscious Framework for Understanding and Addressing Sexual Violence   1
2. Exploring the Contexts of Harmful Sexual Behavior   35
3. Awareness of Sexual Violence Among College Students   63
4. Responding to Sexual Violence Among College Students   81
5. Prevention of Sexual Violence Among College Students   103
6. Strategies for Effectively Addressing Sexual Violence Through a Power-Conscious Lens   131

References   161

ABOUT THE AUTHOR

Dr Chris Linder is Professor of Higher Education in the Department of Educational Leadership and Policy and Director of the McCluskey Center for Violence Prevention at the University of Utah. Chris's scholarship focuses on equity and power in higher education, with a specific focus on sexual violence. Working over a decade as a student affairs practitioner, Chris strives to make her scholarship applicable and accessible to practitioners. She leads research teams that include student affairs practitioners, students, and researchers to ensure that research is relevant and that the implications and recommendations of her research are applicable in higher education settings.

Previously, Chris's scholarship focused on student activism, the developmental processes of anti-racist white women, and the experiences of students of color in student affairs and higher education graduate programs. She has published work in the *Journal of College Student Development*, the *Review of Higher Education*, the *Journal of Higher Education*, and the *Journal of Diversity in Higher Education*. She currently serves as Editor for the *Journal of Diversity in Higher Education*. Chris served on the Board of Directors for the ACPA: College Student Educators International and the Association for the Study of Higher Education.

FOREWORD

I have the kind of job that others tell me, "I could never do that," then quickly change the subject. I often wonder which part seems the most difficult: Is it hearing years' worth of survivors recounting experiences with sexual harm and violence? Is it the parents of the accused who assume I'm out for their child because I simply believed the survivor was telling me their truth? I wonder if it's because of the worry that I am perceived as siding with the accused because I ask, "how can I support you?" Could they "never do" my job because the crisis of sexual violence is too big of a problem and too overwhelming to address? As a Title IX Coordinator engaged in campus sexual violence response and prevention for more than 10 years, I can tell you that all the above and more make my work feel insurmountable. This book is not going to give us the magic answer, and if you're engaged in violence response and prevention, you know the work is far too complicated for such expectations. Instead, Chris Linder implores us to reconsider (or for some, to begin to consider) the relationship *we* – and students impacted by sexual violence – have with power.

In 2017, I picked up a copy of a book Linder coedited, *Intersections of Identity and Sexual Violence on Campus* (2017), and began attending her speaking events or webinars when I could. As a self-proclaimed social justice educator and fellow queer, white, cisgender woman, I admired and felt challenged by the ways Linder called me into accountability as a Title IX administrator on college campuses. Moreover, Linder has consistently called attention to how BIPOC and disabled students experience sexual violence on campus and are often disproportionately accused. All too often, the regulatory world is preoccupied with only monitoring regulations while considering the historical, political, and current social relationships with power as Title IX administrators is seen as a luxury rather than a requirement. By 2018, when the first edition of *Sexual Violence on Campus* was released and I was in the first year of my PhD program, I'd familiarized myself with Linder's research and had begun to develop my own sense that higher education needed to attend to the impact of sexual violence adjudication processes on both complainants and respondents. All-or-nothing policy adjudication not only ignores historical contexts of sexual violence but leaves little, if no, room for administrators to provide resolution processes that meet community needs and educate respondents.

The second edition of Linder's, *Sexual Violence on Campus* comes on the heels of the 2024 Title IX Final Rule which provides that educational institutions can more broadly consider alternative resolution processes among other changes. Chapter 2 of the second edition is new and gives way for coordinators, advocates, and conduct officers to further name the power raging through acts of sexual violence, in our institutions, and even within ourselves. Linder's work has captivated me for many years not only for its resonance, but also as she has challenged me to recognize my relationship to power and grapple with the role we've played in reproducing the carceral state. My first "grappling" with my role in the carceral state was in 2014, as the Director of Student Conduct, when I issued an expulsion letter to a first-year student found responsible for sexual assault. He was Black, an athlete, and the first in his family to go to college. The complainant was traumatized by what happened. The respondent left the institution unable to understand, grow, and repair, but not unwilling. I cried white lady tears on my drive home that day and almost quit my job. This student changed the way I understood my role and continues to challenge me to interrogate how power works in higher education and my complicity in its workings. Linder's work invites us to consider our roles long before I did however. This book is a tool for administrators to interrogate their relationships to power through policy adjudication before we're given the authority to enforce them. In fact, I cannot imagine doing the work as a Title IX Coordinator without committing to a lifetime of re-examining the role I play in reproductions of institutional violence. Engaging in Linder's work and recommendations for change play a significant role in my self-examination.

Because the "power-conscious framework calls attention to the role of power in the individual, institutional, and cultural levels of interactions, policies, and practices, [it necessitates] that the symptoms *and* causes of oppression be addressed. (Linder, 2018, p.14)" Linder makes the case that we must realize our roles beyond compliance and grapple with our relationships to power within our institutions. More specifically, she advocates for a community-based approach that is willing to directly name harm-doing, not just identify who gets hurt. In the spring of 2022, I took this advice to heart and inspired by the first edition of *Sexual Violence on Campus* (2018), received a small grant to host a group of students over a 5-week period to read and engage in dialogue around the book. At the time, I was a Title IX Investigator at a large public institution. Prevention was not formally part of my job description, but because I believe strongly in the role I must play to advocate for change, I hosted this dialogue group. The small group of students and three administrators met weekly.

The experience affirmed my assumption, and Linder's urging, that policies will not change or shift power: our communities together will. Each of the students ended the experience by telling me they wish they'd been able to engage in the work sooner and that all students would benefit from open, transparent, dialogue about power and sexual violence.

Recently, a colleague told me they were struggling with how to not take survivors' and respondents' critiques of the institutions personally. They felt deeply responsible for the betrayal these students felt. In my response, I thought of Linder's work and having recently read this second edition, I responded by saying that we take it personally because we want students to have positive interactions with us as representatives or agents of the systems. However, those systems and our policies don't take power and oppression into consideration. We can't let our desire to be seen as "nice" or "helpful" be the gauge for success and we (Title IX administrators) have set a low bar for ourselves regarding our definitions of "success." I told the colleague that while I believe complainants and respondents are disenfranchised by our systems and policies, that does not mean we get to absolve ourselves of the need to question, push, and ask "can we do this a better way?" Our policies will not save our students any more than they will save us. However, policy development and adjudication without a power-conscious lens and action will cause further harm to students and burn through us. Part of our work must be to recognize our own relationships to power, trauma, and harm and create pathways as campus leaders for our students and communities to do the same. Linder's work provides suggestions for how to do this.

In the second edition of the book, Linder shares her reflections on an abolitionist approach to sexual violence response. She says, "Abolitionist writers and thinkers [...] taught me we must engage in risk-taking and making mistakes in order to eradicate violence" (p. 37). In other words, how can we create campus communities that resist the binaries of responsible or not responsible, and consider harm and trauma that happened, *AND* how we can heal together? As the second edition of this book comes at the time we are asked to revise and reconsider our policies and re-imagine practices in Title IX, we have an opportunity to respond to the community rather than treating incidents of sexual violence as one-time occurrences.

Megan Karbley, PhD (she, her, hers)

PREFACE TO FIRST EDITION

I am a secondary survivor of interpersonal violence. I grew up in a home where men in my life were emotionally, mentally, and physically abusive to my mother and to my younger brother. However, I didn't realize this until well into my twenties. I was in my first job after my master's degree and began volunteering at the local domestic violence shelter. I went to my first training with a van full of other volunteers and remember crying most of the way back from the training because I realized how prevalent interpersonal violence was, so prevalent that I had not even identified it as part of my experience. It was just normalized. If it was normalized for me, how many others were impacted in this way?

Although I was already working in higher education, I was not knowingly or intentionally working with survivors of violence. This quickly changed. I began working with our organization to address sexual violence in fraternities and sororities and started spending more time at the women's center on campus. The director of the women's center saw something in me and mentored me, teaching me about dynamics of power and privilege. She taught me how to work against systems of domination while working in the system. She illustrated how to create a space where people can be their full, authentic selves. The women's center was a place for students on campus who did not feel at home in most other spaces on this traditional, Midwestern campus. The campus was dominated by fraternity and sorority and sports cultures, cultures rooted in white supremacy and patriarchy; the women's center was a place where queer, feminist students of color could build community and live fully.

Eventually, I left this institution to work in a women's center in another state, where I spent the bulk of my student affairs career. I directed a center that managed a 24-hour-crisis hotline for survivors of sexual assault; provided educational programs for faculty, staff, and students; and developed a variety of programs to address inequity in higher education. Throughout my time in this center, I grew in my understanding of power and privilege, specifically related to the intersections of race and gender. I pursued a PhD and wrote my dissertation about the developmental processes of undergraduate white feminist women striving to engage in racial justice. I further developed my own, more nuanced racial consciousness and feminist, queer identity. Building on what I learned from my experience in the Midwest, I listened to and learned from students and colleagues of color and worked to create a space where people could come and be their full, authentic selves. Our center also became a space for many students who did not feel comfortable in other spaces on campus and provided an opportunity for them to build community with each other.

In addition to serving as a space for queer, feminist student of color to gather and build community, our center was also the primary support program for survivors of sexual violence on campus. We provided advocacy and support for survivors as they navigated the aftermath of sexual violence, including reporting to campus or criminal punishment systems if they so chose. We also educated faculty and staff on campus about how to appropriately support survivors of sexual violence. Our center was the hub on campus for interpersonal violence and we were frequently pulled in numerous directions to support and advocate for survivors of interpersonal violence throughout campus.

As a staff member and director in a campus-based victim advocacy center, I felt the urgency of the problem of addressing sexual violence on college campuses. I heard stories on a daily basis of people experiencing violence, and I often felt overwhelmed and hopeless. I felt as though I was just spinning my wheels, constantly responding to crises, rather than figuring out ways to stop violence before it started. As with most centers, we were understaffed and overworked, and because we were ultimately a crisis center situated in the identity-based cluster (e.g., multicultural centers, LGBT center, and disability services) of a division of student affairs, we had little support in terms of supervision related to crisis and violence. I struggled to figure out the balance of confidentially supporting survivors while also engaging in strategies to address interpersonal violence and to support other centers in their work toward equity.

Eventually, I saw that I was dealing with my own secondary and vicarious trauma and realized it was time for me to move on from crisis work. I left my position at the women's center and became a full-time faculty member in a higher education program. For the first few years of my faculty career, I did not engage in work related to sexual violence. I needed time to heal from my experience in crisis-related work. Of course, I kept an eye on what was happening related to campus sexual violence, and in Fall 2013, I noticed that the momentum related to addressing campus sexual violence was shifting dramatically. I was pulled back into sexual violence work, this time as a researcher. After taking some time to heal, I was ready to re-engage. In the Spring of 2014, I assembled a research team to examine the strategies of sexual violence activists. We wanted to know what was causing the shift in momentum around the issue of campus sexual violence. Engaging in this research also led me to examine the role of power and privilege in sexual violence work, specifically as they relate to race and racism. We sent a call for participants to our national networks in the United States, including several national grassroots organizations that had been organizing college students over the previous several months. No Black or Indigenous activists chose to participate in our study, despite our efforts to intentionally contact some activists we knew identified as Black or Indigenous. Upon further reflection and additional research about campus activism, I learned that many people of color do not consider themselves "activists," rather they see their work as a responsibility or obligation to their communities. Further, some people in racially minoritized groups see their work as essential to their survival, not a choice or an activity in which they engage.

During this time, I also had a realization about my role as a former campus-based advocate turned faculty. After taking some time to heal from my own vicarious trauma, it was time for me to get back to work – this time in a new way. Faculty has unique power on campuses: we can say things that practitioners cannot say for fear of losing their jobs or experiencing significant consequences. We can challenge notions of tradition and usually are not caught up in the day-to-day crisis work in which many prevention and response professionals find themselves. We can name that reactive policy is actually distracting us from the larger work of eradicating sexual violence on college campuses. Writing this book is one strategy in which I am engaging to attempt to contribute to the eradication of sexual violence on college campuses. Using my unique position as a former campus-based sexual violence advocate and a current researcher dedicated to examining power and oppression in campus environments, I strive to interrupt and name power dynamics in sexual violence prevention and response and provide strategies for addressing sexual violence from a power-conscious perspective.

ACKNOWLEDGMENTS

Although I have spent a lot of time and energy in my professional career and personal life thinking about ways to more effectively address sexual violence, the ideas I share in this book are in no way exclusively mine. My thoughts about sexual violence and more effectively addressing it have developed over time through trial and error in my own practice, conversations with critically minded friends and colleagues who share my passion for eradicating violence, and by reading and attending conferences with many brilliant minds. I do my best to appropriately cite information as I know it, and I am sure that I have missed some important work here. Information about campus sexual violence is coming in a record number of ways (e.g., blogs, videos, reports, published journal articles and books) and exponentially faster than at any other point in our history. For these reasons, and because of my own limited perspective, I am confident that I have missed some very important resources and contributions to the work of eradicating sexual violence on college campuses. Even still, I share my thoughts with you as a contribution to the on-going important work and hope that it reaches some people at the right time and the right place in their lives to make a difference.

As I engage in the work of coming to better understand power, privilege, and oppression, I acknowledge the labor (often unpaid) that women of color, trans folks, and people with additional minoritized identities do to educate me – a queer white cis woman – about oppression. A considerable amount of my learning about oppression related to racism, genderism and ableism, among other systems of domination comes from "nonacademic" (e.g., not published in journal articles and featured at academic conferences) spaces, including blogs and online media. I cite many of these works throughout this book because I want other people who work in traditionally academic spaces to examine these perspectives, rooted in people's lived experiences, as legitimate forms of knowledge. As illustrated throughout this text, we (those of us who work on college campuses) would make a lot more progress eradicating the work of sexual violence if we listened to more than just each other. Abolitionist thinkers and writers – in particular Mariame Kaba, Andrea Ritchie, Adrienne Marie Brown, Ruha Benjamin, Danielle Sered, and Susan Raffo – have deeply informed my growth and thinking over the past few years.

I am also grateful for the time, energy, and expertise of close colleagues and friends who have contributed to my thinking about ending violence. I am deeply grateful for the wisdom and compassion of Drs Niah Grimes and Nadeeka Karunaratne who have been my thought partners, coauthors, mirrors, editors, and confidants for the past year. We have done our best to practice abolition by creating the communities we want to live in and loving on each other through the good and the bad. Additionally, Dr Meg Evans, Whitney Hills, Jilly Mcbane, and April Pavelka read and provided feedback on chapters in this book, and I am grateful for their wisdom and expertise.

I am also grateful to the current and former student and core staff members at the MCVP who have pushed my thinking in many ways and made me a better leader. They try their best to keep me up to date on the latest lingo and technology and help me see the world more clearly. The staff have listened to my musings and reflected back to me what made sense and what didn't. They do their best to interpret my wacky ideas, make them better, and most importantly, JUST TRY. I have learned so much over the past five years leading this Center, and it is because of the courage of the people who work here to "just try" and see what happens. Failure is part of the process, and we've embraced that. We've had some failures, and we've had far more successes. We embrace the mess and do our best to create a community of love, joy, and resistance. We speak up when we experience harm, and we take responsibility when we cause harm. It has been a beautiful space, and I am grateful to the people who have made it what it is.

INTRODUCTION

Writing the second edition of this book is illuminating in a number of ways – and indicative of our ability and need to continually evolve. As I reread these chapters to think about ways that things have changed since the first edition of the book, I note that the most significant change happened in me, not the context in which we work. As much as the world, and more specifically my context in the United States has changed in the past six years, it has also stayed largely stagnant around addressing issues of sexual violence among college students. We are surviving a global pandemic and have had some major (and temporary) reckonings around racism and police violence. College students appear to have more awareness related to mental health, disability, and gender identity. Students do not shy away from identifying as disabled, and in fact, some refer to it as a badge of honor (Stanek & Mattson, 2024). More college students come to campuses identifying as genderqueer, interrupting traditional notions of gender identity (Beemyn, 2022). They are proficient on social media, using it to both raise awareness with each other about common social problems and identity, as well as to educate themselves on meal prepping and finances (Hosie, 2020). This generation of students pushes educators and administrators to be more cognizant of caring for students' whole beings and expects us to take care of ourselves as well. More students push back on traditional notions of "work" and "success" than ever have before (Hall, 2024).

At the same time, the United States is incredibly divided. People have the least faith they have ever had in higher education (Brenan, 2023). People – college students included – tend to be more divided on social issues than ever before (Dimok & Wike, 2020), resulting in campuses being challenging places to engage in dialogue focused on learning and development. As more students become aware of issues related to power, privilege, oppression, and identity, they have less patience for their peers who are not on board with their perceptions and arguments. At the same time, students (and parents and politicians) who feel threatened by discussions related to power and identity push back through legislation prohibiting attention to issues of "equity, diversity, and inclusion" on college campuses (Flannery, 2024). This divided world makes discussions related to power very difficult. Many of us have internalized messages that we need to dig our heels in, advocate staunchly for our "right" position without pausing to consider others' perspectives and experiences and where our perspectives might overlap. Others of us have internalized the message that we need to be careful, resulting in us not pursuing conversations with a variety of perspectives.

In terms of my own development over the past six years, I have spent a considerable amount of time digging into and understanding abolitionist organizing principles. I have sought to better understand carcerality, carceral feminism, and my investment in these practices. I have founded and direct a Center focused explicitly on the primary prevention of dating and sexual violence among college students. I have hired and supervised staff, interns, and researchers, attempting to build collaborative community wherever possible.

I have also struggled with the tensions inherent in community building around an issue that impacts so many of us and that people have dramatically different philosophies for engaging. I hold strongly to the belief that sexual violence prevention and response should be separated for reasons I describe in this book. I further believe that all forms of oppression are connected, as also illustrated throughout this book. I know that there is overlap between the ways that people in larger communities experience sexual violence and the ways that college students do. That said, I also believe that we all have limited resources and expertise. For this reason, I maintain tight boundaries around maintaining a focus on sexual violence prevention among college students. As a leader of a sexual violence prevention and education center, this means that we say no to awareness-raising events like tabling. It means that we don't partner with every community organization that focuses on sexual violence. It means we say no a lot more often than we say yes. This can be uncomfortable. As people who do work related to social justice issues, we have been taught to say yes to everything – to accept every partnership, every collaboration, and every opportunity to "get our name out there." I am not always popular, yet I believe strongly in the idea that rest is resistance (Hersey, 2022) and that we all only have so much energy to give. When we say yes to everything, it can distract and take away from the work that we have said that we contribute to the movement. If I say yes to this, it means I must say no to that. And vice versa. As someone committed to community, these boundaries can sometimes feel uncomfortable – and I know I don't always get it right. That said, I hope these boundaries allow other people to consider their own boundaries and to be clear about the contributions they make to the work. We can support each other's work without collaborating on it – in fact, we may be more supportive by saying no to collaboration and yes to showing up. When we can't do all the things we say yes to, we end up causing frustration in the long run. "No." is a complete sentence.

ORGANIZATION OF THIS BOOK

The purpose of this text is to advance a power-conscious lens to challenge student activists, administrators, educators, and policymakers to develop more nuanced approaches to sexual violence awareness, response, and prevention on college campuses. In Chapter 1, I provide an overview of the framework of the book, including a power-conscious framework and a description of the awareness–response–prevention trifecta of addressing sexual violence on college campuses. In Chapter 2, I examine perpetration and harm in the context of historical trauma, dominance, and oppression. In Chapters 3, 4, and 5, I examine the current state of awareness, response, and prevention of sexual violence on college campuses, interrogating current practices through a power-conscious lens. In Chapter 6, I conclude with strategies to more effectively develop synergy between awareness, response, and prevention strategies, identifying some potential power-conscious approaches for addressing sexual violence among college students.

1

DEVELOPING A POWER-CONSCIOUS FRAMEWORK FOR UNDERSTANDING AND ADDRESSING SEXUAL VIOLENCE

ABSTRACT

In this chapter, I share the power-conscious framework as a tool for examining sexual violence among college students. The framework consists of three assumptions: power is omnipresent, power and identity are inextricably linked, and history matters. The framework includes six action-oriented tenets: (a) engage in critical consciousness and self-awareness; (b) consider history and context when examining issues of oppression; (c) change behaviors based on reflection and awareness; (d) name and interrogate the role of power in individual and systemic practices; (e) divest from privilege; and (f) work in solidarity to address oppression. I also share definitions of words used frequently throughout the book.

Keywords: Power-conscious; sexual violence; college campus; prevention; awareness; response

The term *power* is frequently associated with sexual violence prevention and response, yet rarely defined or examined. In fact, power is a ubiquitous term that means different things to different people. Power can be used for good, bad, or some murky combination of the two. Generally, for the purposes of this book, I use the word power to refer to the ability to control or significantly influence other people's lives. Power frequently comes in two forms: formal and informal.

Formal power includes positional roles that influence other people's lives. For example, in many cases, supervisors and managers have control over employees' work schedules, salaries, and work environments. Similarly, legislators and other policymakers influence people's lives by developing and implementing educational, health, and economic policies. Finally, police, judges, and prosecuting and defending attorneys have power in criminal punishment systems. These individuals have significant discretion to influence people's lives and well-being related to law and law enforcement.

Closely related to formal power, informal power also influences people's day-to-day lives. Informal power refers to the ability to influence or control something without a formal title or role. Some people have informal power over others based on social identities and systems of oppression (Johnson, 2006; Tatum, 2000). Social identities include the identities given meaning through social constructions assigned to those identities, including race, gender, sexual orientation, and ability among others. Systems of oppression include things like racism, sexism, homophobia, genderism and transphobia, classism, and ableism, among others. These systems give members of dominant groups (e.g., white, middle- and upper-class, nondisabled, and cisgender people) access to resources based on social norms and expectations (Johnson, 2006; Tatum, 2000). For example, because cisgender people are considered the norm in relationship to gender identity, policymakers set up policies and practices that center cisgender people's comfort, including so-called bathroom bills that prohibit transgender people from using restrooms aligning with their gender identity. Transgender people, on the other hand, experience higher rates of violence in public spaces, including restrooms, schools, and workplaces because they do not always fit societal definitions of the norm (Bagagli et al., 2021). Similarly, white people frequently have access to greater forms of power than people of color with similarly situated identities. What I mean by this is that white middle-class men typically have greater access to power than middle-class men of color. This informal power results in access to institutions and resources, assumptions of "goodness," and ultimately greater access to safety and security.

How does power relate to sexual violence? Examining histories of sexual violence in western countries points to a number of ways that power is the root of sexual violence. Specifically, when Europeans colonized Indigenous lands in what is today considered North and South America, they used rape as a tool of power and control (Deer, 2015). Colonizers raped Indigenous people as a way to reward themselves for conquering villages and to keep Indigenous people living in fear so that white colonizers could better control them (Deer, 2015; Freedman, 2013).

Similarly, slavers used rape as a tool of power and control over enslaved people. Because the children of enslaved women became the property of the slave-owner, slavers frequently raped enslaved women as a way to increase their labor supply and economic power (Freedman, 2013). These two examples illuminate some of the roots of the relationship between power and sexual violence – roots that continue to grow deeper over time. In the US postemancipation, white men, especially those with formal and institutional power like police, used rape as a tool to keep formerly enslaved people "in their place" (McGuire, 2010). By raping Black and Indigenous people with impunity, white men demonstrated their power to control other people's lives and create a sense of fear in minoritized communities (McGuire, 2010; Thompson-Miller & Picca, 2017). White, owning-class men used rape as a tool of domination by falsely accusing Black men of raping or attempting to rape white women. In the period postemancipation, white men mobbed and lynched Black people at alarmingly high rates, often in relationship to false accusations of rape (Giddings, 1984; McGuire, 2010).

Patterns of domination and control continue today. People who cause sexual harm target women of color, gay and bisexual people, transgender people, and people with disabilities at higher rates than their white, straight, cisgender, and nondisabled peers (Cantor et al., 2019; Coulter et al., 2017), likely because minoritized people's very existence threatens the comfort and perceived safety and security of dominant group people. Members of dominant groups have an investment in the status quo because they benefit from the ways systems are currently structured, including the ability to cause harm to people without fear of repercussion.

LANGUAGE CONSIDERATIONS

The language of sexual violence is complicated and nuanced and varies depending on context. For the purposes of this text, I define *sexual violence* as any act of nonconsensual physical sexual assault or rape, including nonconsensual touching. Although some scholars use the phrase sexual violence to encompass sexual harassment (including verbal harassment and hostile environments), I am concerned about conflating physical and nonphysical sexual harm. Although acts of nonphysical sexual violence certainly lead to physical sexual violence, and the consequences of nonphysical sexual violence are significant, my concern about conflating the two relates to numbers. The reality is that almost every person who identifies as a woman or nonbinary person has experienced verbal sexual harassment at some point in their lives, in some cases, almost daily (National Sexual Violence Resource Center, 2019; UCSD Center, 2019). By conflating sexual harassment and sexual assault, I worry that scholars and activists dilute the significance of physical sexual assault and contribute to the narrative that women and nonbinary people are overexaggerating their experiences because we are not using accurate language to describe those experiences.

Although I use the term sexual violence to refer to physical sexual assault, I realize that not all research does the same; therefore, as I refer to other people's work and scholarship on sexual violence and assault, I will do my best to clarify what definitions other scholars use. For example, scholars use the terms *unwanted sexual touching*, *sexual coercion*, *incapacitated rape*, *forcible rape,* and *sexual assault* to examine and discuss prevalence of sexual violence. Each of these terms has specific definitions that may or may not be the same across the research. To minimize confusion among people taking surveys about sexual violence, many researchers ask about specific behaviors, rather than specific terminology, then categorize the behaviors into various terms (deHeer & Jones, 2017; Wood et al., 2017).

Additionally, because of the heavy emphasis on compliance with policy mandates as explored in Chapter 4, many discussions on sexual violence focus on illegal behavior rather than harmful behavior. As Levine and Meiners (2020) note,

"'Crime' is a legal category and a volatile, malleable political term. 'Harm', on the other hand, is a relationship and experience[...]'harm' allows people to name and describe what happened to them" (p. 7). For these reasons, throughout the book, I focus on harmful behavior rather than just illegal behavior.

Scholarship about sexual violence frequently centers gender in its analysis; however, most scholars use binary language when examining gender and frequently focus on *men* or *women* in their scholarship (Linder et al., 2020). Although scholarship about sexual violence must examine constructs of gender as they relate to sexism, patriarchy, cissexism and other systems of oppression, scholars must also work to intentionally include expansive notions of gender in their work. For example, throughout this book, when I refer to *women* or *men*, I am referring to all people who identify as *women* or *men*. A gender expansive definition of *women* or *men* refers to people who align their identity in some way with the constructs of women or men and includes cisgender and transgender people. Additionally, some people do not identify with the constructs of men or women, and instead, identify as a nonbinary gender or with no gender at all (i.e., agender). People who identify with a nonbinary gender may use terms like *gender nonbinary*, *genderqueer*, *gender nonconforming*, and/or *transgender* to describe themselves. Throughout this book, I will use the term *gender nonbinary* to refer to people who do not identify with the constructs of the binary of woman or man. I do not use the phrase *men and women* in my work. The phrase is simply inaccurate – it excludes people who identify as nonbinary or genderqueer. Instead, I simply use the word *people*. If I am specifically referring to cisgender or transgender men or women, I will explicitly name that.

Additionally, I use the term *minoritized* to refer to populations of people who have experienced harm as a result of systems of oppression and domination. While some scholars have historically used the term *minority* to refer to populations of people who experience oppression and marginalization, I find the term *minority* inaccurate because it refers to a numerical representation of people when that is not always the same as experiencing systematic oppression. For example, in the US, women make up more than half of undergraduate students on campus (National Center for Education Statistics, n.d.), so they are not in the numerical minority; however, given the culture on college campuses, they still experience significant harm as a result of sexism, which is an example of a system of oppression.

The term *system of oppression* refers to the systematic ways people experience harm and violence as a result of power, privilege, and domination (Collins, 2000; Johnson, 2006; Tatum, 2000). Examples of systems of oppression include racism, sexism, homophobia, and ableism. Referring to systems of oppression rather than the minoritized group puts the onus on the problem – oppression – rather than the people experiencing the problem. For example, scholars consistently examine the experiences of people of color in education, calling attention to ways students of color experience higher education differently (often more negatively) than their white peers, yet fail to name racism as the cause of these negative experiences. Failing to name the system of oppression as the problem contributes to a deficit perspective on people of color in education, highlighting the ways in which they do not "succeed" in the same ways as their white peers (Harper, 2012; Patton, 2016).

Taking the problem of identifying and naming actors responsible for sexual violence one step further, I also use active voice as frequently as possible in this text. Active voice puts responsibility on people for perpetuating oppression and harm (Lawrence et al., 2019). When discussing sexual violence, scholars and journalists frequently make people who cause harm invisible. For example, phrases like "women of color are assaulted at high rates" removes any actor from the discussion. Who is responsible for the action of sexual assault? Using phrases like "people who cause harm target women of color at high rates" puts the onus on the people who cause harm and subtly calls attention to addressing the problem of sexual violence by emphasizing the role of people who cause harm *and* naming the harm caused to victims.

In the first edition of this book, I referred to perpetrators throughout the text. Since writing the first edition, I have shifted my way of thinking away from using the phrase perpetrator to *people who cause harm*. Sometimes, I use the term *people who cause sexual harm, or people who have or may cause harm* or *people who have engaged in sexual violence*. All of these terms describe the behavior a person engages in rather than describing the person as the problem. As described in the introduction, I have become more in tune with abolitionist thinking as a way to eradicate sexual violence, and abolitionist thinking requires us to recognize that no human is disposable (Kaba & Ritchie, 2022). Instead of referring to a person by the most harmful behavior they have engaged in, we can begin to see people who cause harm as human beings with the capacity to change when we focus on the behavior, rather than labeling the person as the problem (Willis, 2018). Although I do not use the term perpetrator in this text, I do sometimes use the term *perpetration* to describe the set of behaviors associated with causing sexual harm. To me, there is a difference between referring to a person as a perpetrator and referring to the behaviors associated with perpetration.

As I have engaged in abolitionist thinking, I have also changed my language from referring to the *criminal justice system* to the *criminal punishment system*. Although people invested in the status quo would like us to believe that the legal systems in which we exist bring justice, that is seldom the case. As I will explore more in Chapters 2 and 4, many survivors are asking for accountability over punishment (Decker et al., 2022; Gartner et al., 2024; Ratajczak & Wingert, 2024), and our current legal systems prioritize the opposite. Legal processes center punitive responses to violence, which only begets more violence (Sered, 2019). To accurately represent this, I use the phrase *criminal punishment system* to describe current legal processes. Similarly, I use the phrase *carcerality* or *carceral practices* to refer to the overall system of surveillance, control, and punishment (Kaba & Ritchie, 2022) integrated into almost every aspect of our lives.

Finally, I often use first-person language in this text so that I don't distance myself from the problems being addressed. Although I historically discouraged the use of the words such as *we, our,* and *us* in academic writing because they can be unclear referents, I have recently shifted my perspective. Many writing constructions are a result of white supremacy culture (Okun, 2021; Radical Copy Editor, n.d.), and I often participate in those constructions. As I continue to evolve as a thinker and writer, I have begun to interrupt some of those habits. Using first-person language is one way to interrupt white supremacy culture in writing; including myself as part of the problem and solution is important. Additionally, although I may make assumptions about who is reading this book by using *we, our,* and *us*, I also think it is important to build community around this work, trusting that most of us who work in higher education have the intention to eradicate sexual violence, even if our strategies for doing so may look different.

In the remaining part of this chapter, I describe the development of a power-conscious framework to examine issues of sexual violence on college campuses and describe a trifecta of awareness, response, and prevention that guides many campus leaders' strategies to address sexual violence.

BUILDING A POWER-CONSCIOUS FRAMEWORK

A power-conscious framework requires scholars, activists, educators, administrators, and policymakers to consider the role of power in individual, institutional, and cultural levels of interactions, policies, and practices. Identity and power are inextricably linked, so power-consciousness also requires attention to identity. I developed a power-conscious framework by reading and reflecting on the work of previous critical scholars and activists, including work about critical consciousness (Friere, 2000; hooks, 1994) and intersectionality (Crenshaw, 1989, 1991).

Although some tenets of a power-conscious framework are rooted in similar assumptions as intersectionality, a power-conscious framework is broader than intersectionality. Scholars created intersectionality to center the experiences of women of color and their experiences with systems of domination and oppression (Collins, 2000; Crenshaw, 1989, 1991). Using intersectionality in other contexts risks misappropriating the scholarship (Harris & Patton, 2019). I do not intend to use a power-conscious framework *in place of* intersectionality or to indicate that intersectionality *only* focuses on race and gender. Centering racism in the examination of sexual violence warrants increased attention from researchers and activists and will certainly be a part of the examination of power in this book. However, far too many white people – and white women specifically – have misappropriated and misused intersectionality by using it to examine oppression broadly rather than focusing explicitly on racism and sexism and their varied intersections (Harris & Patton, 2019). I use a power-conscious framework to call attention to dominant group members' investment in power rather than attempting to center and speak for women of color. Prior to describing a power-conscious framework, I provide a brief overview of critical consciousness and intersectionality.

Critical Consciousness

Largely rooted in her work on engaged pedagogy, bell hooks (1994) builds on the work of Paulo Freire to advocate for critical consciousness among feminist scholars and activists. Specifically, Freire (2000/1970) describes the process of conscientization or the ways members of minoritized groups must come to see and understand the ways oppressors have taught members of minoritized groups to accept their status as the oppressed group. Using both consequences for acting out *and* teaching people to accept their role in systems of oppression, oppressors have successfully built systems that benefit themselves and harm everyone else (Freire, 2000/1970; Tatum, 2000). Freire calls for an awareness of oppression coupled with action based on this awareness, or praxis, as part of a critical educational process.

hooks (1994) builds on Freire's work, calling attention to the ways teachers and students must develop a deeper understanding of their own experiences with oppression and the ways they also oppress others. hooks (1994) calls on people focused on critical education and scholarship to engage in deep reflection and consciousness-raising related to their own experiences with oppression as they intersect with systems of power and domination, including the "white supremacist, capitalist, patriarchy" (hooks, 1994, p. 26). A critical consciousness, including self-awareness and an awareness of systems of domination, is the foundation of a power-conscious framework.

Intersectionality

Rooted in critical legal studies, intersectionality calls on scholars to examine the intersections of oppression – namely racism, sexism, and classism – to more deeply understand and address the ways women of color experience oppression and harm (Crenshaw, 1989, 1991). Kimberle Crenshaw (1991) advanced an intersectional framework specifically as it relates to white feminists' erasure of women of color in movements to address interpersonal violence, including sexual assault.

Crenshaw (1989) uses the court's response in the case of *DeGraffenreid vs General Motors* (GM) to illustrate the significance of the intersections of systems of domination for women of color, specifically Black women. Five Black women filed suit against GM in 1977 for discrimination based on sex and race because GM failed to promote Black women into senior leadership positions in the organization. The court granted summary judgment to GM, arguing that white women and Black men had been promoted within the organization, which illustrated that sexism and racism did not influence promotion practices at GM. The summary judgment based on the experiences of white women and Black men rendered the experiences of Black women invisible. As Crenshaw (1989) argued,

> *The court's refusal in* DeGraffenreid *to acknowledge that Black women encounter combined race and sex discrimination implies that the boundaries of sex and race discrimination doctrine are defined respectively by white women's and Black men's experiences. Under this view, Black women are protected only to the extent that their experiences coincide with those of either of the two groups. (p. 59)*

In 1991, Crenshaw further drew on her analysis of the *DeGraffenreid* case to illustrate the ways feminist organizations and legal systems ignored women of color in responding to interpersonal violence (Crenshaw, 1991). Crenshaw highlighted structural, political, and representational intersectionality to illustrate this erasure.

Structural intersectionality illustrates the ways social location influences people's experiences with oppression. The "location of women of color at the intersection of race and gender" makes their experiences of sexual violence "qualitatively different than that of white women" (Crenshaw, 1991, p. 1245). Interpersonal violence directed at women of color is not only gendered but also raced. Women of color not only navigate sexist oppression but also racialized sexist oppression, including a number of stereotypes and experiences of harm directly related to their racial identities. For example, people who cause harm may view multiracial women as exotic, Latina women as "hot and spicy," Black women as jezebels, and Asian women as exotic and passive (Harris, 2017), resulting in different experiences with sexual violence than their white women peers.

Political intersectionality highlights the reality that people may experience competing agendas at the intersection of their identities. For example, given the racism *and* sexual violence directed at women of color by police (Ritchie, 2017), women of color may not trust the criminal punishment system or people acting on behalf of the criminal punishment system. However, most interpersonal violence response systems organized on college campuses or through community agencies include a primary relationship and focus on police (Goodmark, 2022; Kim, 2018). Different from their white women peers, women of color must balance the tension between reporting experiences of sexual violence to police with the risk that they will experience harm at the hands of police (Goodmark, 2023; Wallace et al., 2024).

Finally, representational intersectionality refers to the "cultural construction of women of color" (Crenshaw, 1991, p. 1245), or the master narratives created without women of color about their experiences. An example of representational intersectionality exists in the professionalization of interpersonal violence response systems. As with most activism around issues of social justice, Black women originally led movements to address interpersonal violence, including organizing grassroots community organizations to support survivors of interpersonal violence (Bevacqua, 2000). However, as these community organizations became more dependent on funding from foundations, grants and governmental organizations, they also began to "professionalize" and integrate more with mainstream response systems (e.g., criminal punishment systems) as a form of legitimization (Kim, 2018, 2020). This professionalization of interpersonal violence response took away from the feminist, grassroots, community organizing feel of the work (Bummiller, 2008; Incite, 2006; Kim, 2018, 2020). Today, many community-based agencies and interpersonal violence response organizations fail to hire women of color into leadership positions, contributing to issues presented here related to representational intersectionality.

THE POWER-CONSCIOUS FRAMEWORK

Building on the work of critical consciousness and intersectionality scholars, a power-conscious framework requires that scholars, activists, and educators maintain an awareness of the role of power in addressing issues of oppression. Centering the experiences of minoritized communities is essential in justice and equity work and so is calling attention to the ways in which power contributes to the organization and maintenance of oppression. Systems of oppression operate by maintaining the status quo, by attempting to make people believe that if they work hard enough, that if they change themselves enough, they too can be successful in current systems. A power-conscious framework challenges scholars and activists to reconsider current structures and to consider ways for dismantling and restructuring systems to share power rather than building structures that contribute to one group having power over another group. Some feminists have borrowed from the business management literature and refer to this idea as a "power with" rather than "power over" perspective (Boje & Rosile, 2001, p. 106).

Activists and educators frequently focus on the needs of minoritized communities and people who are harmed by oppression and rightfully so. Focusing on the needs of and listening to people with minoritized identities is essential for dismantling systems of oppression. However, oppressors maintain systems of oppression by busy-ing people, especially people with minoritized identities, with focusing on addressing the symptoms and outcomes of oppression, rather than addressing oppression at its roots. If oppressors can keep oppressed people busy and preoccupied with taking care of each other and attempting to break into the structures that currently exist, then oppressors do not have to change their behavior or the systems that benefit them.

A power-conscious framework calls attention to the ways power works and requires that people not only address the symptoms of oppression but also the causes of oppression. For example, on college campuses, some faculty and staff spend a considerable amount of time, energy, and resources supporting students of color students who do not feel welcome, valued, seen, or heard on their campuses. Faculty and staff may also spend time and energy teaching students with minoritized identities to figure out how to assimilate and fit into the structures that exist on campus. Although support for students navigating a hostile campus climate is an essential role for faculty and staff, so is interrupting and changing the systems that currently exist, the systems that make it so that students with minoritized identities must navigate a hostile environment. A power-conscious framework requires that scholars and activists draw attention to the power and structures that exist rather than focusing exclusively on addressing the symptoms of oppression. What if educators and activists spent time, energy, and resources engaged and intervening with white students who perpetuate racism, along with supporting students experiencing racism? Similarly, with sexual violence work, what if institutional leaders spent equal resources intervening with people engaging in sexually violent behavior rather than *only* teaching potential targets of violence how not to be victimized?

Focusing on the response to the problems of oppression is easier than addressing the roots of oppression because focusing on the roots requires addressing and altering power. For example, when addressing sexual violence at the roots, people must interrogate, name, and challenge oppression, including racism, sexism, homophobia, transphobia, ableism, and others. Naming oppression and power requires making people with dominant identities uncomfortable, and they will likely resist this discomfort. Acknowledging that sexual violence is about oppression and the interlocking systems of it, rather than about people's bad decisions related to alcohol, requires that people understand, acknowledge, and *change* their behaviors complicit with oppression. Similarly, acknowledging the role of power in sexual violence requires that people hold their loved ones accountable to consider that people – especially cisgender men – in their families and friend groups may have caused harm or engaged in sexual violence toward another person.

A power-conscious framework pushes scholars and activists to address both the symptoms *and* the roots of oppression, not one or the other. In the following sections, I describe the assumptions undergirding the framework and the six pillars of the framework (see Fig. 1).

Assumptions

Several assumptions undergird a power-conscious framework: power is omnipresent, power and identity are inextricably linked, and history matters. First, power is omnipresent, meaning that power is present in every interaction between individuals and between individuals and systems. No interaction is power-neutral and no policy or practice is devoid of power. As described above, power is both formal and informal, meaning that people have access to power because of position or authority or because they are perceived as the norm or default in a society. For example, a teacher has power over a student based on their position (formal power). Similarly, cisgender people have power in relationship to transgender people because they are considered the norm when it comes to gender identity (informal power). Cisgender people's gender and gender presentation align with their sex, making members of the dominant group – cisgender people in this case – comfortable.

18 Sexual Violence on Campus

POWER-CONSCIOUS FRAMEWORK

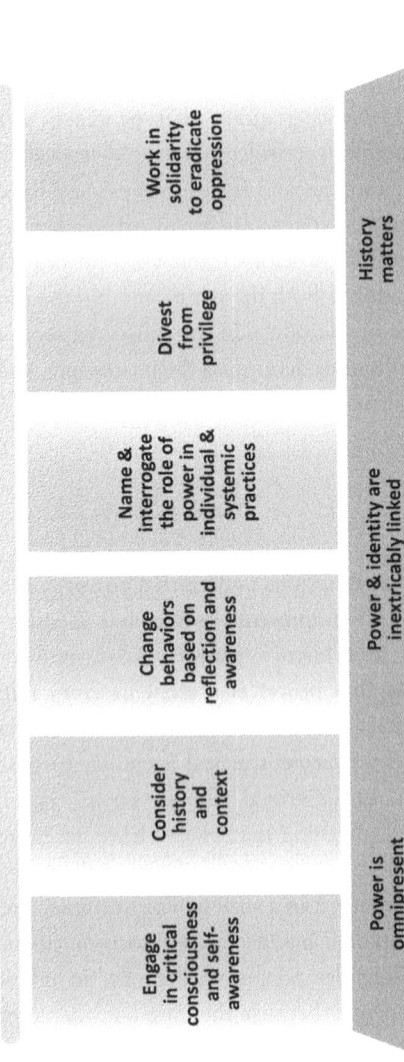

- Engage in critical consciousness and self-awareness
- Consider history and context
- Change behaviors based on reflection and awareness
- Name & interrogate the role of power in individual & systemic practices
- Divest from privilege
- Work in solidarity to eradicate oppression

FOUNDATIONS & ASSUMPTIONS

- Power is omnipresent
- Power & identity are inextricably linked
- History matters

Fig. 1. Power-Conscious Framework.

Second, power and social identities are inextricably linked. Social identities include the identities given meaning through social constructions assigned to those identities, including race, gender, sexual orientation, and ability, among others. Although people with common identities share some characteristics, the meaning associated with those characteristics is constructed. For example, white people throughout history have organized people into racial categories based on phenotypical features such as skin color, hair texture, and eye shape and have assigned meaning to these racial categories (Omi & Winant, 1994). Throughout history, white men determined that people with dark skin were inferior in intelligence to people with light-colored skin. White men constructed intelligence quotient (IQ) tests by writing questions that white men excelled at answering. They validated IQ tests by administering them to white men and when white men did not do well on particular questions, those questions were thrown out (Gersh, 1987). Using white men as the default group on which to measure IQ leads to people of color and women and nonbinary people's experiences and perspectives being considered inferior.

One of the challenges in understanding the significance of the relationship of power and identity is that people in minoritized communities have also assigned meaning to their identities as a form of resistance. Dominant groups – primarily white, cisgender, heterosexual, and nondisabled men – have created and codified power in relationship to identity (Tatum, 2000). Additionally, members of minoritized groups have used the organization of socially constructed identities to exercise agency through the power they gain by being in community with each other. For example, although people with power have determined that gay, lesbian, bisexual or queer people are different and inferior to heterosexual people, LGBQ people have come together to attempt to reclaim power taken away from them by people with power. Being in community with other people who share a common identity deemed negative by dominant groups results in a shared sense of purpose, pride, and solidarity, which results in people being empowered to show up and live full, authentic lives. Because members of minoritized groups have also created meaning around their identities, sometimes members of dominant groups have a difficult time understanding how identities are socially constructed because they are unaware of the history described here.

The social construction of identities leads to the third assumption undergirding a power-conscious framework: history matters. The meaning assigned to identity has been developed and codified over time. As outlined by critical race theory scholars, ahistoricism contributes to continued racism because people attribute oppression to modern-day policies and practices, rather than understanding the significance of the ways oppression has been historically interwoven into policies, practices, and systems (Delgado & Stefancic, 2012). As illustrated by the examples above, oppression has deep roots in the construction of educational practices (e.g., IQ tests), laws (e.g., allowing only opposite-sex couples to legally wed), and practices (e.g., requiring victims of violence to formally report to police to access victim services). Oppression is not a modern-day invention and cannot be eradicated overnight. To engage from a power-conscious framework, scholars and activists must examine and understand history from a critical perspective, then work to interrupt oppression.

Tenets of a Power-Conscious Framework

The underlying assumptions of a power-conscious framework lay a foundation for the tenets of a power-conscious framework or the pillars that interconnect to uphold the framework. Tenets of a framework provide an organized way for scholars and activists to interrogate or analyze an idea, phenomenon, policy, or practice to improve them for future use. For this reason, the tenets of the power-conscious framework are action-oriented, requiring active engagement from scholars and activists. Further, the tenets of this framework also provide some guidance for people to continually engage in action to dismantle systems of oppression. The processes of awareness and action are mutually reinforced and must be done together. Too often, I hear people engaged in social justice work express that they are afraid to do anything because they do not "know" enough. Although it is important for people to be thoughtful and intentional in their social justice work to avoid causing harm, we can also never know enough – we must act, learn from our action(s), and act again.

The first three tenets of the power-conscious framework require scholars and activists to engage in personal reflection and growth and the second three tenets require us to move toward collective action. The tenets include: (a) engage in critical consciousness and self-awareness; (b) consider history and context when examining issues of oppression; (c) change behaviors based on reflection and awareness; (d) name and interrogate the role of power in individual and systemic practices; (e) divest from privilege; and (f) work in solidarity to address oppression.

Engage in critical consciousness and self-awareness. One of the primary foundations of critical, power-conscious work is developing a critical consciousness and engaging in self-reflective behaviors. Self-awareness requires people to be aware of who they are and how they show up in a space. Self-awareness is especially important for people with dominant identities because those of us with multiple dominant identities (e.g., white, educated, cisgender, and nondisabled people) frequently do not notice the ways people with minoritized identities experience the world. For example, as a neurotypical person, I sometimes fail to consider the ways students and colleagues with whom I work navigate anxiety and depression and how current structures for academic work privilege neurotypical people. We are frequently more self-aware related to our experiences with minoritized identities because we constantly need to think about the ways we navigate the world not set up with us in mind. For example, as a woman, I am highly cognizant of gendered microaggressions and structural sexism because they negatively impact my life daily.

Self-awareness is critical for developing a critical consciousness or an awareness of the role of power in everyday actions and in systems. A critical consciousness does not necessarily mean that a person constantly criticizes or looks for the negatives in every situation; rather, a critical consciousness means that a person considers how something may be harmful to another person or exclude people from having access to essential needs to live a safe and fulfilling life. Developing a critical consciousness requires people to consider structural as well as individual level practices and their role in those practices. Building on my example above, after realizing how my neurotypically focused advising practices and expectations for writing impacted some advisees with whom I worked, I adjusted my approach to advising, providing more structured support for students who needed or wanted it. Similarly, I have adjusted my teaching pedagogy on more than one occasion as I have become aware of ways that traditional classroom practices privilege neurotypical people and harm neurodivergent people. For example, I stopped using case studies that students needed to read in class because people with learning disabilities and people for whom English is not their primary language have shared that reading case studies in class creates a sense of overwhelmedness and does not allow them to fully participate in the learning.

People engaged in social justice work have long advocated the significance of self-awareness (Goodman, 2012) and critical consciousness (hooks, 1994) as a significant part of the process of working toward equity and social justice. Unfortunately, many people translate the significance of self-awareness and critical consciousness as the end point rather than the starting point of social justice work. Further, some people begin the process of developing a critical consciousness, then get so overwhelmed by their understanding of oppression and the significance of it, that they feel immobilized. Some people may also experience an incredible "fear of doing it wrong" that also immobilizes them. People engaged in social justice work must work through these barriers.

Consider history and context when examining issues of oppression. Oppression does not happen in a vacuum and did not emerge overnight. Ahistoricism, or the failure to consider how people with power engrained systems of oppression into the fabric of systems, policies, and practices, leads to ineffective strategies for addressing oppression (Delgado & Stefancic, 2012). For example, sexual violence laws in the US first emerged as property crime laws. White, owning-class men were the only people who could file sexual violence charges in the 17th and early 18th centuries (Donat & D'Emilio, 1992; Freedman, 2013; Lindemann, 1984). If their wives or daughters were raped or sexually violated, men could claim that their property had been violated. Courts and legal systems did not allow women to own property or have any legal standing, so only men could make a claim related to the sexual violation of women (Freedman, 2013). Although this law has changed today, understanding the significance of it in history helps to better understand and point out sexism in the legal system and the relationship between power and ownership.

Our experiences with oppression vary depending on the contexts in which we exist, so when using a power-conscious framework, we must consider the context in which we work. Context includes the political and cultural environments in which we exist, as well as the ethos of a particular campus or community. As it relates to addressing sexual violence among college students, a campus's culture around risk is particularly salient. As the regulations related to the interpretation of Title IX continue to morph and change, some campus leaders subscribe to a conservative approach to their interpretation, erring on the side of reducing their risk of federal fines, while other leaders employ a less risk averse approach. Compelled disclosure policies are an example of this. Some campus administrators interpret the law as requiring every faculty and staff member on campus, regardless of their training, to be a mandatory reporter, requiring them to notify a Title IX official of any report of potential sexual misconduct. Other campus administrators may follow a less risk averse approach to the interpretation of the guidelines, carving out more opportunities for confidential spaces on campus for survivors to share their experiences without triggering a report to a Title IX official (Holland et al., 2018). While many people who work on campuses understand there to be a national guideline for interpretation of Title IX, there is significantly more room for legal interpretation than most of us realize.

Change behaviors based on reflection and awareness. After we develop a practice of self-awareness, critical consciousness, and an awareness of history and context, we must engage in action that reflect this awareness. Simply being aware of oppression and privilege is not enough. Awareness is an essential starting place because we cannot act if we do not understand the depth and nuance of a problem. Developing a critical consciousness and self-awareness and a deeper understanding of history and context requires an on-going commitment to learning at the same time we engage in action (Freire, 2000/1970; hooks, 1994). As described above, we sometimes fail to act because we feel like we do not know enough or are afraid or overwhelmed, and this behavior (or lack thereof) contributes to continued oppression of people with minoritized identities. For example, if I regularly observe racial microaggressions in my faculty meetings but feel afraid that I might use the wrong words to name the microaggressions so I don't speak up, the microaggressions are likely to continue. We must change our own behaviors when we know and understand differently. As Maya Angelou said, "Do the best you can until you know better, then do better." If we know that we are complicit in oppression, yet do nothing to interrupt it, we are a part of the problem.

Similar to how self-awareness is an important first step of critical-consciousness, individual-level change is an important first step in systemic change. For example, once we know that people who cause harm target people with minoritized identities (e.g., women of color, people with disabilities, and queer and trans people) at higher rates than their dominant group peers (Cantor et al., 2019), we should change our language from saying "she" when referring to people targeted for sexual violence to simply saying "victim" or "person targeted for violence" to illustrate that women are not the only people targeted for sexual violence. Similarly, in educational and resource materials, we should be mindful of the photos we use and the messages we send about who targets of sexual violence are. Rather than only using photos of typically attractive white women, often perceived as heterosexual and cisgender, we should strive to represent a wide variety of people in our materials.

Name and interrogate the role of power in individual and systemic practices. As we pay attention to and begin to change our own behaviors based on our awareness and reflection, we must facilitate this change beyond ourselves. By externally naming the ways we observe power showing up in individual and systemic practices, we begin to move beyond ourselves to interrupt systemic oppression. Consistently asking questions like "Who is centered in this program/policy? Who is erased or ignored through this program/policy?" "Who does this policy exclude, intentionally or unintentionally?" "How are power structures developed and sustained in this work?" and "What is the impact of power (or lack thereof) on people's real and lived experiences?" may lead to a deeper awareness of the role of power in well-intended programs and practices.

Given that higher education is in a state of crisis when it comes to sexual violence, institutional leaders frequently search for, and are bound by, one-size-fits-all policy mandates. Unfortunately, most of these mandates, like most policy, privilege dominant group members (Anderson Wadley & Hurtado, 2023; Roskin-Frazee, 2020). Addressing sexual violence at its roots – entitlement and power – requires a nuanced approach not available through one-size-fits-all policy and practice. For example, many institutions have adopted a one-time bystander intervention online education program that all students must complete prior to enrolling in college. Bystander intervention programs rest on a foundation of community care and the idea that people in community want to take care of each other (Banyard et al., 2004). The assumption that campuses are a "community" may be flawed. Students' perceptions of who is worthy of protecting from sexual violence vary based on race; white women are less likely to intervene in cases where the potential victim is a Black woman (Katz et al., 2017), largely because many white women do not see Black women as part of their community, the very foundation on which bystander intervention rests. Interrogating the role of power in bystander intervention programs may lead some educators and activists to make different decisions about effective sexual violence prevention programs.

Another way systems disproportionately favor people with dominant identities is by continuing to center dominant group members' comfort at the expense of people with minoritized identities' safety. Awareness programming frequently focuses on the number of people assaulted in an academic year. What if instead of *only* focusing on the number of victims who experience sexual violence, we also focused on the number of people engaged in harmful behavior and the frequency of their behavior? How might violence prevention change if educators and activists focused on changing the behavior of people who engage in harmful behavior rather than *only* the behavior of potential victims? What if we made people who engaged in harmful behavior visible in our statistics by including things like, "one in seven college men has engaged in behavior that meets the legal definition of sexual assault" (Gidycz et al., 2011)? Naming and turning power on its head is one strategy for interrupting the ways that power is routinely ignored in our "best practices."

Divest from privilege. In addition to becoming aware of the influence of power on individual and systemic practices, people using a power-conscious framework must intentionally divest from privilege in many ways. Because systems in their current form prioritize people with dominant identities, people with dominant identities are frequently invested in the maintenance of those systems, albeit sometimes subconsciously. Although most dominant group members would not explicitly say that we are invested in the maintenance of these systems, our behaviors indicate otherwise, and as mentioned before, the intersections of dominant and minoritized identities make this investment even more complicated. For example, because white middle-class people have been taught that the criminal punishment system works well, many white middle-class women invest in upholding the authority of the criminal punishment system even though it actually harms many of us when it comes to issues of interpersonal violence. Investment may include continuing to work with and trying to incrementally change the criminal punishment system rather than attempting to work completely outside the system to address issues of violence.

Similarly, because white women often benefit from white male privilege because of our close relationships to white men through marriage or as our fathers, we also invest in upholding systems of white male supremacy because it benefits us in the short run by making our personal lives easier and richer (Hurtado, 1996). Divesting ourselves of this privilege requires significant shifts in our ways of thinking and behaving. One of the biggest stumbling blocks to interrupting dominance is people with privilege resisting discomfort. When we are accustomed to being centered in every process and procedure, it might feel uncomfortable to listen to and learn from people with different experiences than us. Divesting from privilege requires that we pay attention to what is going on around us and take seriously the feedback provided to us by people with minoritized identities where we have privilege.

Work in solidarity to address oppression. None of us is solely responsible for oppression, and all of us are responsible for eradicating systems of domination. When we examine our relationships to power and dominance, we can get hung up on whose responsibility it is to end different kinds of oppression. While there is certainly some value in people with dominant identities being invested in uprooting oppression related to those identities, it can also be limiting to have only people with dominant identities engaged in the work of uprooting oppression because we have a less nuanced understanding of the ways that type of oppression impacts people who experience it.

In recent decades, well intended "male feminists" have attempted to engage in the work of teaching other men to recognize their privilege and to interrupt oppression wherever possible (Peretz, 2023). Similarly, white people organizing and engaging each other in anti-racist discussion groups strive to reduce some of the labor on people of color who frequently engage in educating white people about racism. Unfortunately, if not done in collaboration with members of the groups who experience oppression in these identities, these groups may cause more harm than good. In addition, people with dominant identities (i.e., "male feminists" and "anti-racist white people") tend to receive excessive amounts of praise for very little work and change (Peretz, 2023).

Abolitionists teach us to focus on working in community with one another to eradicate oppression (Kaba & Ritchie, 2022). Recognizing that we all have unique gifts and talents that we bring to anti-oppression work allows us to divide labor based not only on experiences with oppression but also the gifts and talents that we bring to a space. By focusing on the ways that people think about and show up in the work, rather than *only* on people's identities, we make more progress. This still requires that people, especially people with dominant identities, pay attention to the ways we have been socialized to show up in organizing spaces as "leaders" in a very traditional sense yet also recognize the many kinds of labor that needs to be done and divide it accordingly. For example, while it is important for someone to be responsible for taking notes at meetings and coordinating follow-up communication, it is equally important to ensure that this labor does not fall to only the women in the group based on stereotypes and assumptions about women's roles in groups. Similarly, setting up and cleaning up meeting spaces is important, and it is important to ensure that this responsibility does not fall solely to the people of color in the group based on stereotypes about race, class, and physical labor.

Working in solidarity with one another, taking turns, tagging out when exhausted, and holding each other accountable in social justice work are vital. When gatekeepers determine whose role it is to do what work, it is likely that they are passing over people with exceptional talents and skills. Additionally, for some people, working with and educating oppressors is part of their healing process, and gatekeepers should not be responsible for determining who gets to do what. For example, if a survivor has worked to heal from their experience with sexual violence, they may want to begin to work with people who cause harm as part of their ongoing healing and activism. Professional gatekeepers should not tell them they cannot do this; rather, people can step in and out of engaging in different roles to address oppression over time. Telling people what they should and should not do based on their identities and experiences further contributes to paternalism and on-going oppression, especially as it relates to minoritized identities.

Three underlying assumptions and six tenets provide a framework for approaching the eradication of sexual violence through a power-conscious framework. In the next section, I describe a framework for understanding the current practices related to addressing sexual violence on college campuses (see Fig. 2).

Fig. 2. Awareness–Response–Prevention Trifecta.

AWARENESS–RESPONSE–PREVENTION TRIFECTA

Although campus activists have been challenging university administrators to effectively address sexual violence among college students for decades, in recent years attention to sexual violence has grown exponentially (Martinéz-Aleman & Marine, 2023; Prior & deHeer, 2023). As I reflect on what I have observed over the past few decades related to sexual violence among college students, I see scholars, activists, educators, and administrators striving to address sexual violence from three overlapping perspectives: awareness, response, and prevention. Scholars, activists, educators, and administrators can use the synergy of these three perspectives to effectively eradicate campus sexual violence. I represent these perspectives as three overlapping rings in a Venn diagram.

The *awareness* ring refers to the ways in which scholars, educators, and activists attempt to bring the problem of sexual violence into the consciousness of administrators and students. Awareness frequently consists of activists letting others know of the significance of sexual violence through sharing statistics about the rates of sexual violence and facts about the consequence of sexual violence, including the ways survivors of sexual violence experience trauma and the significant financial costs of sexual violence to institutions and individuals. Similarly, educators and advocates also attempt to raise awareness about the significance of sexual violence on college campuses and resources to support survivors in the aftermath of sexual violence.

The *response* ring of the trifecta refers to the ways institutional agents (faculty, staff, and administrators) address sexual violence after it happens. For example, response includes services for victims of sexual violence like counseling and support for navigating criminal punishment systems. Response also includes the adjudication processes that attempt to hold people who cause harm accountable for sexual violence, with the intention of reducing rates of sexual violence. Similarly, some campuses provide support and assistance for the families and friends of survivors of sexual violence in the aftermath of violence.

Finally, the *prevention* ring refers to the strategies institutions employ to address sexual violence before it happens. Prevention strategies may include both risk reduction and interrupting harm. Risk reduction focuses on teaching people how to avoid experiencing harm, helping them identify signs of violence, and avoiding or leaving a situation that might become harmful or violent. Interrupting harm focuses on stopping violent or harmful behavior before it ever happens. From a power-conscious framework, risk reduction is not actually violence *prevention* – it is violence re-organization.

Reducing one's risk of experiencing violence may result in a person not experiencing violence in one particular instance, but it does not stop a person who may cause harm from engaging in the behavior. If we do not intervene with and stop people from engaging in harmful or violent behavior, we are just shifting the harm and violence somewhere else. Violence prevention means stopping a person from engaging in harmful or violent behavior altogether, not just in one instance.

Some strategies represent overlap between two or three rings of the trifecta. For example, educational workshops frequently fall into the prevention and awareness categories – educational workshops attempt to both raise awareness about the problem and provide some strategies for reducing the risk of sexual violence. An example of a strategy that falls into the middle is an education program that lets students know about the significance of the problem of sexual violence (awareness), teaches students how to respond if a friend discloses to them that they have been sexually assaulted (response), and discusses the nuances of receiving consent for sexual activity (prevention).

In the following chapters, I explore the context in which violence happens and then examine current practices on college campuses in each of the three rings through a power-conscious lens. I conclude the book with a chapter highlighting strategies that may more effectively address campus sexual violence.

2

EXPLORING THE CONTEXTS OF HARMFUL SEXUAL BEHAVIOR

ABSTRACT

In this chapter, I examine contexts in which harmful sexual behavior occurs. I identify current perceptions about harmful sexual behavior, including ways researchers engage in research about harmful sexual behavior, and carceral approaches to addressing harmful sexual behavior. I then examine oppression as the root of violence, highlighting the relationship between dominance, oppression, violence, and trauma. I conclude the chapter by suggesting strategies to engage people who engage in harmful behavior in accountability and healing.

Keywords: People who cause harm; harmful sexual behavior; carceral practices; accountability; trauma

Since writing the first edition of this book, our collective desire to better understand harmful sexual behavior and people who engage in harmful sexual behavior has grown stronger. Many of us actively question why we continue to put responsibility on people targeted for violence to stop something from happening to them rather than engaging with people who have or may cause harm to get them to disrupt and change their behaviors. We question why rates of sexual violence among college students have not budged for decades (Muehlenhard et al., 2017) and seek more complex and nuanced responses to eradicate violence. In this chapter, I add to the discussion about interrupting harmful behaviors by examining our understanding (or lack thereof) of harmful sexual behavior and offering some emerging thoughts about why some people may engage in harmful sexual behavior. Considering different reasons people engage in harmful sexual behavior will help us create better tools to stop those behaviors.

I feel anxious writing this chapter, about putting my ideas about perpetration, harm, and people who cause harm into the world for many reasons. Over the past few years, as I have started to explore harmful sexual behavior by focusing on the people causing harm, I have experienced resistance from my feminist colleagues and friends. In fact, when presenting at a feminist conference in 2022 with two colleagues, a participant in the session berated us for having compassionate responses for those who cause harm. Not only did this person, who I perceived to be a white woman, become verbally aggressive with all of us, but she physically intimidated one of my colleagues, who is a younger Black femme academic. The encounter was traumatic for my colleague and certainly illustrated some of the risks of engaging in this work, along with a whole host of other things about white supremacy culture at "feminist" conferences.

Like many of us, I have been heavily socialized into being "victim-centered," which in our zero-sum world, frequently translates to ostracizing people who cause harm. Carcerality has led us to believe that we must punish people who cause harm and that by humanizing them, we are somehow minimizing or disbelieving victims' experiences (Kaba & Ritchie, 2022). I am also anxious to put my ideas into the world because they are still forming. We know little about harmful sexual behavior from research, and the research we do have is mired in dualistic assumptions, which I explore more below. By the time this book is published, I'm sure my thinking about harmful sexual behaviors will have already shifted.

Survivors of interpersonal violence and abolitionist writers and thinkers have helped me move through this fear to contribute to the conversation about harm and violence. The number of survivors I have sat with over the years who have said, "I don't want them to get in trouble - I just want them to stop" pushed me to think differently about the carceral mentality we have collectively adopted in our culture as it relates to addressing harm. Many survivors do not want to engage punitive, carceral approaches to addressing harmful sexual behavior – they want more complex responses than we currently have (Decker et al., 2022; Gartner et al., 2024; Ratajczak & Wingert, 2024). Some survivors *implore* us to focus on people engaged in harmful behavior and to better understand harmful sexual behavior. Further, abolitionists challenge us to recognize that no human is disposable and that ending violence requires that we engage with people who have caused harm to help them understand and change their behaviors (Brown, 2020; Kaba & Ritchie, 2022). Abolitionist writers and thinkers have also taught me that we must engage in risk-taking and make mistakes in order to eradicate violence (Hayes & Kaba, 2023). My ideas are far from complete; yet, given my experiences and protection from losing my job as a tenured professor, I have a responsibility to push us forward – to put ideas into the world that may generate additional thinking.

I organize this chapter by examining current perceptions about harmful sexual behavior and then examining oppression as the root of violence. I conclude the chapter by examining potential strategies for addressing harmful sexual behavior through a power-conscious framework.

PERCEPTIONS ABOUT HARMFUL SEXUAL BEHAVIOR

Scholars, activists, and victim advocates have examined and described sexual violence, including sexual assault, stalking, intimate partner violence, and other forms of violence for decades. Advocacy around sexual violence has ebbed and flowed over time, with Black and Indigenous women leading resistance movements for centuries in what is now referred to as the US (McGuire, 2010). While our collective understanding of survivors' experiences of sexual violence has grown over time, we have less knowledge and understanding of people who engage in harmful sexual behavior. Many things contribute to our collective lack of understanding; to contextualize this chapter, I focus on two: dualistic and binary thinking about violence and misperceptions of people causing harm.

Dualistic and Binary Thinking About Violence

While scholars and activists tend to agree that sexual violence happens when some people choose to exercise power and control over other people, we have a less clear understanding of the dynamics of power. The relationship between power and sexual violence is nuanced and complex. In mainstream US culture, we tend to oversimplify concepts associated with power to make sense of the complexity. Often, we discuss power as something that we have or we don't have, yet the reality is much more complex. Our relationships to power are contextual, changing depending on our relationship to other people in the spaces in which we find ourselves. For example, as a white cisgender middle-aged woman faculty member on my campus, in most rooms I find myself in, I hold incredible power and privilege. People listen to me because I look like what they expect education professors to look like: a middle-aged white woman. That said, when I shift my location and go to a meeting of upper-level administrators (acknowledging the level of privilege it requires to even be invited into that space), my relationship to power suddenly shifts. I am one of very few women in the space and I am a "soft" scientist. As a result, I am less likely to be heard and more likely to be written off as that "wacky woman who has weird ideas about addressing sexual violence." In the same space (my home campus) in different locations, my relationship to power is different.

Similarly, the role of power in sexual violence is also nuanced and contextual. We often talk about how people engage in harmful sexual behavior because they have/are enacting power over others. This is true, *and* it's more complex than just "power over" someone. Power shifts, depending on the identities and positionalities of people involved in a situation. White feminism has, for decades, constructed sexual violence as always already gendered, resulting in perpetuation of gender as the primary factor the around which the study of sexual violence has been organized. When I refer to white feminism in this context, I am referring to the *political identity* of white feminism (see Schuller, 2021), which constructs feminism as singularly focused on gender or sexism. White feminists have constructed sexism as the primary contributing factor to sexual violence, resulting in an inaccurate depiction of sexual violence which oversimplifies our approach to addressing violence.

Given that people who cause harm target people with minoritized identities, including women of color, queer and trans people, and people with disabilities, at higher rates than their peers (Cantor et al., 2019; Coulter et al., 2017; Griner et al., 2020), we must examine sexual violence through a more complex lens than a gender binary. Research about sexual violence rarely interrogates identities beyond binary sex, providing little understanding of the experiences of students of color, students with disabilities, and students with additional minoritized identities (Harris et al., 2020; Klein et al., 2021; Linder et al., 2020). Further, even when research centers students with minoritized identities, researchers often fail to employ a framework that examines power to make sense of the findings. Instead, they use instruments and frameworks developed with dominant group members' experiences to measure the experiences of students with minoritized identities (Linder, Caradonna, et al., 2024).

Even when researchers examine "gender," they only examine binary sex. For example, in one study that examined 454 articles published over a 10-year period, only 1.4% of the reviewed articles asked about nonbinary identities. Additionally, most research about perpetration focused on men and the research about victimization focused on women (Linder et al., 2020). These implicit assumptions about the gendered nature of sexual violence are replicated repeatedly, resulting in research that "mutually constructs" itself (Harris et al., 2020, p. 27). When research starts with the assumption that men perpetrate and women experience sexual violence, we end up knowing little about any other kind of violence, and gendered assumptions are consistently reinforced.

In addition to the binary nature of gender, discussions about sexual violence often revolve around a binary or dualistic perception of victims and perpetrators. Many education and intervention programs, as well as policies related to sexual violence, assume a victim-perpetrator binary, failing to account for how some people might be both someone targeted for violence *and* someone who engages in violent or harmful behavior. Given the exceptionally high rates of violence in our culture, including childhood sexual abuse, the number of people who have both experienced harm and perpetuated harm are quite high (Gámez-Guadix et al., 2011). Experiencing violence is a significant risk factor for perpetuating sexual violence (Gray et al., 2017; Kettrey et al., 2023). The dualistic nature of thinking about victims and perpetrators contribute to less than effective strategies for intervening with those who cause harm and for understanding the complexities of harmful sexual behavior. Closely related to the dualistic and binary ways of thinking about violence, another challenge in our understanding of harmful sexual behavior are the misperceptions and misrepresentations of harmful sexual behavior in our culture.

The Misperceptions of Harmful Sexual Behavior

More people are beginning to recognize that we need to understand why people engage in harmful sexual behavior so that we can stop it from happening in the first place. Unfortunately, a lot of our culture's understanding of harmful sexual behavior is inaccurate, largely rooted in misperceptions of crime, which is tied up with racism, classism, homophobia, and additional forms of oppression. The misperception of harmful sexual behavior contributes to ineffective strategies for ending and understanding harmful sexual behavior, as illustrated in the examples below.

To start, our language contributes to a stereotypical representation of harm. Frequently, we refer to people who engage in harmful sexual behavior as *perpetrators* or *sex offenders*. When you think of a sexual assault perpetrator or a sex offender, who or what comes to mind? What about when you hear the term *person who engaged in harmful sexual behavior*? Unfortunately, for most of us socialized in dominant US culture, the images are likely vastly different. The image of a *perpetrator* frequently brings to mind a dark-skinned, strange man wearing a ski mask or hoodie to conceal his identity, often lurking in the dark waiting for an innocent woman to pass so that he can attack her (Colburn & Melander, 2018; Patton & Snyder-Yuly, 2007). Similarly, the term *sex offender* frequently brings to mind someone who has engaged in childhood sexual abuse (Levine & Meiners, 2020). The term *person who has engaged in harmful sexual behavior* may be more less aggressive and imply lack of intent or knowledge of the harmful behavior.

The reality is that all three ways described here happen; however, most sexual harm is perpetuated by people we engage with on a regular basis throughout our lives, not strangers (Cantor et al., 2019; Whynacht, 2021). A long history of racism, classism, and homophobia contributes to our collective construction of a perpetrator or sex offender. In fact, illustrating that "race in America is the foundational arbiter of sexual innocence and guilt" (Levine & Meiners, 2020, p. 41), most laws, policies, and practices related to addressing sexual violence perpetuate racist thinking.

Dating back to emancipation, white people constructed formerly enslaved Black men as perpetrators of violence, claiming that they preyed on innocent white women in sexualized ways (Freedman, 2013; McGuire, 2010). Various evolutions of the racialized representation of men of color as perpetrators have evolved over time, with perceptions of racialized crime sealing the passage of the Violence Against Women Act in the height of the "tough-on-crime era" of the 1980s and 1990s (Goodmark, 2021; Kim, 2018). Similar to how research mutually constructs itself to perpetuate a binary gendered way of thinking about sexual violence, policy, legal, and criminal punishment systems engage in cycles that perpetuate racist, classist, and homophobic ways of thinking about sexual violence. When policymakers start with an assumption that people who engage in harmful sexual behavior are poor and/or of color and/or queer, laws and the enforcement of these laws focus on these populations. Although people with minoritized identities are not more likely to engage in harmful behavior, they are more likely to be criminalized for it. People of color, poor and working-class people, and queer people are over-represented in the criminal legal system, including jails and prisons (Nellis, 2021). However, it is not because people with these identities commit more "crime"; it is because police target marginalized communities for enforcement and judges and juries are more likely to find people with minoritized identities responsible for engaging in "criminal" behavior. I use quotation marks to describe crime and criminal behavior because the construction of crime in US culture is arbitrary, with laws intentionally targeting specific people for "criminal" behavior when the exact same behavior is considered appropriate in other communities (Kaba & Ritchie, 2022; Vitale, 2017). For example, what makes something loitering rather than gathering with friends in a public place?

Media representations of harmful sexual behavior also contribute to misperceptions. Scholars refer to the racialized representation of crime in the media as the "missing white woman syndrome," which describes the way that media outlets frequently spend more time and energy focused on missing or murdered white women than other people who experience crime (Rosner, 2021). Similarly, media outlets frequently over-report crimes perpetrated by people of color, and include photos when the person committing the crime is a person of color, but not when the person is white (Colburn & Melander, 2018). In the 1980s, at the height of the "tough-on-crime" era, fear of "stranger danger" also escalated, especially related to the abduction of children (Levine & Meiners, 2020). The media covered the reports of missing children, but rarely the safe return of children. In fact, in 2018, of reports of "missing children," 95% ran away from home – they were not abducted by strangers. Of the 5% that did not run away, most were illegally taken by a noncustodial parent (Reuters, 2019). The focus on sex offenders as a major problem in our culture has resulted in six federal laws between 1994 and 2016 designed to eradicate childhood sexual abuse (Levine & Meiners, 2020). Even though 90% of sexual abuse directed toward children is perpetrated by family members and close family friends, the laws target "stranger danger" (Levine & Meiners, 2020, p. 45).

On college campuses, similar dynamics exist. Most sexual violence that happens on college campuses happens between two people who know each other (Cantor et al., 2019). As you may also recognize, most prevention or risk reduction strategies propagated on college campuses focus on stranger danger (Bedera & Nordmeyer, 2015) or stereotypical sexual violence involving fraternity men, athletes, and alcohol (Kettrey et al., 2023). Blue light systems, walking with a friend, carrying mace, and taking self-defense classes all focus on "stranger danger" or someone jumping out of the darkness to attack an innocent person. Similarly, bystander intervention programs focus on teaching students to be aware of potential harmful behaviors which are often rooted in stereotypical understandings of sexual harm, even when not intended to be so. While research indicates that hyper-masculinity perpetuated by all-male social groups is a risk factor for sexual violence and alcohol exacerbates risk factors for engaging in sexual violence (Gray et al., 2017; Spencer et al., 2022), overly focusing on stereotypical instances of sexual violence results in less complex understandings and approaches to addressing violence.

Research about harmful sexual behavior on college campuses is also limited, and as highlighted above, likely "mutually constructs" (Harris et al., 2020, p. 27) itself. Although an in-depth examination of the role of assumptions in research, especially research about sexual violence, is beyond the scope of this chapter, research about sexual violence is far from unbiased or objective (Harris et al., 2020; Linder et al., 2020; Linder, Caradonna, et al., 2024). Most scholarship about sexual violence among college students employs quantitative methodologies (Harris et al., 2020; Linder et al., 2020). Quantitative research, usually conducted with positivist or postpositivist epistemologies, frequently starts with a hypothesis, which is just a fancy way of saying "set of assumptions." The hypothesis, often rooted in the findings of previous scholarship, is not something that a researcher sets out to "prove" as is commonly accepted but rather, disprove. Researchers can only disprove hypotheses, resulting in us actually "knowing" very little about topics examined in postpositivist research. Further, although previous scholarship informs the development of new hypotheses to examine sexual violence, previous scholarship was designed with an often unquestioned set of assumptions. Often, those assumptions were rooted in dominant paradigm perspectives about sexual violence, which stem from the racist, classist, homophobic policy and legal perspectives and media representations described above. It is perhaps no wonder then that most research about harmful sexual behavior examines the same constructs over and over. Most research centers assumptions rooted in individualistic behaviors about violence (e.g., narcissism, hostility toward women, rape myth acceptance, and alcohol abuse) rather than an understanding of structural oppression. Our collective socialization to postpositivist, quantitative research as the "gold standard" for research has led to inconclusive understandings about harmful sexual behavior, frequently rooted in stereotypes and assumptions, rather than deep and nuanced understanding of why people engage in harmful behavior.

To more effectively prevent violence from happening in the first place, we must engage with a more robust understanding of harmful sexual behavior and find some middle ground between "he just did not know what he was doing" and "the stranger in the bushes" beliefs about harmful sexual behavior. What if we examined harmful sexual behavior as the outcome of a combination of histories of trauma and systems of oppression, which lead to lack of empathy and understanding of other human beings? Our current carceral strategies for responding to violence in dehumanizing ways only beget more violence (Sered, 2019; Whynacht, 2021). In the following section, I synthesize and explore scholarship about histories of trauma and systems of oppression to contribute to a larger conversation about the relationship between trauma, oppression, and violence.

OPPRESSION IS THE ROOT OF VIOLENCE

In our book, *Thinking Like an Abolitionist to End Sexual Violence in Higher Education* (2024), Nadeeka Karunaratne, Niah Grimes, and I highlight the idea that oppression is the root of violence as a key principle of abolitionist thinking. Oppression frequently results in trauma and unhealed trauma frequently results in enacting harm on other people (Menakem, 2017; Raffo, 2022). When we say that "oppression is the root of violence," a person could interpret that to mean that people with minoritized identities (i.e., those who experience systemic oppression) cause harm. While that might be true – some people with minoritized identities engage in harmful behavior – a significant number of cisgender and heterosexual white men enrolled in college who have not experienced as much oppression as some of their peers have engaged sexual violence (Swartout et al., 2015; Zinzow & Thompson, 2015). One of the common factors underlying harmful behavior is unhealed trauma, which emerges from white supremacy culture and dominance.

Intergenerational trauma from violence lives in all of our bodies, including those of us socialized in white bodies. White Europeans used violence, which creates trauma in our bodies, to control other white Europeans for centuries, and people who colonized what is now the US brought that trauma with them, enacting it on people with less power than them (Menakem, 2017; Raffo, 2022). White Europeans observed and survived violent persecution for centuries before fleeing Europe to colonize North America. While historians describe colonizers as "explorers," Menakem (2017) argues that they were not explorers, but "refugees fleeing imprisonment, torture, and mutilation" (p. 60). He explains, "when the English came to America, they brought much of their resilience, much of their brutality, and[...]a great deal of their trauma" (Menakem, 2017, p. 61). White colonizers constructed whiteness as a way for them to maintain dominance to "sooth the dissonance that existed between more powerful and less powerful white bodies" and to enact violence on non-white bodies (Menakem, 2017, p. 63).

Raffo (2022) similarly argues that "Europeans brought their wounds from across the ocean," enacting violence through colonization and genocide (p. 34). Their wounds included a "sense of disconnection" from the land and themselves so that they could enact violence (Raffo, 2022, p. 34). Oppression results in disconnection between the "self with the self, the self with community, and the self with the land and spirit" (Raffo, 2022, p. 26). This disconnection is often a result of trauma, and for people socialized into dominant bodies, that trauma lives in their bodies and is not easily identifiable because they do not experience systemic oppression – in fact, they enact it. The relationship between trauma and systems of oppression may be far more complex than we typically describe. Not only do people with minoritized identities experience oppression and trauma as a result of the dominance enacted by white cisgender wealthy men, but people with dominant identities are likely acting on generations old unhealed trauma still living in their bodies.

The History of Dominance and Oppression

Although a complete history of the relationship between dominance and oppression is beyond the scope of this chapter (or book!), it is important to highlight the ways that people with power intentionally constructed systems that perpetuate dominance and oppression to maintain power and control. The colonization of what is now referred to as the US (and other colonized cultures) wove dominance and control into the very fabric of our culture. When European colonizers came to what is now referred to as the US, they claimed to seek refuge from religious persecution in England yet rebuilt the very same systems of power and control they sought to escape when they established the colonies of the US (Menakem, 2017; Raffo, 2022). Colonizers brought with them the concept of ownership, which was not part of the cultures of

Indigenous people who thrived prior to colonizers coming to the land now referred to as the US (Raffo, 2022). Indigenous people worked *with* the land and with other living beings on the land to ensure that everyone had what they needed to thrive and that land was cared for. Colonizers brought with them "their understandings of private property and land ownership" along with the "separation they had already learned on the lands where they began" (Raffo, 2022, p. 13), resulting in exploitation of both land and people and laying the groundwork for the ongoing violence and destruction we still experience today.

Constructing laws, practices, and values that dehumanized Indigenous and African people allowed white colonizers to exploit and enact violence on Black and Indigenous people. Not only did these laws, practices, and values result in white colonizers becoming rich through the exploitation of Black, Indigenous, and other people of color, they also set the stage for ongoing domination of nonwhite and nonmasculine people (Raffo, 2022; Takaki, 2023). Rather than creating systems where people shared equally in the resources of the land, colonizers sought to hoard resources, resulting in some people having more than they needed and others never having enough (Raffo, 2022; Takaki, 2023). Equally concerning as hoarding resources was the dehumanization of people who did not fit into colonizers' perceptions of who was "worthy" of resources. White colonizers dehumanized Black and Indigenous people, referring to them as uncivilized savages, making it easier for white colonizers to control people of color through violence (Takaki, 2023). The dehumanization of other people required white colonizers to disconnect from their own humanity as well. To enact violence, they had to see themselves as different from or better than the people they enacted violence on and to disconnect from any empathy for other humans they had (Menakem, 2017). The material benefits of capitalism clearly favor wealthy white men and harm most everyone else. However, the harm of capitalism does not stop there. Capitalism, greed, dominance, and oppression also harm people with substantial access to material benefits (i.e., wealthy white men) by requiring them to disconnect from their own feelings, their own humanity, and the humanity of others. The "original wounds" of ownership and exploitation of land and people must be healed to eradicate violence enacted by humans (Raffo, 2022, p. 16). Understanding the relationships between trauma, oppression, and violence allows us to approach violence prevention from a more holistic perspective, working to engage people engaged in harmful behavior in their own healing from isolation and disconnection.

Although it is important to understand the ways that trauma may show up in all our bodies, including privileged white bodies, it is equally important to understand that "trauma is not destiny" (Menakem, 2017, p. 83). People can and do choose to heal their traumas so as not to enact violence on other people. Further, not all people who experience trauma enact violence. That said, better understanding trauma and *all* our relationships to it may contribute to a deeper and more nuanced understanding of why people engage in violence, including sexual violence. A deeper, more nuanced understanding of violence and why people engage in it gives us more options for intervening with people who cause harm to prevent future harm, and to create opportunities for healing as a strategy for preventing violence from happening at all.

In the following sections, I examine two interconnected ways that systems of oppression, created and maintained by people with unhealed trauma, contribute to violence: (1) by setting up binaries, individualism, and competition and (2) by facilitating dehumanization, disconnection, and isolation.

Binaries, individualism, and competition. Systems of oppression require binary thinking: one is either deserving of privilege or not. People with power constructed laws, practices, and values in a way that people are considered bad or good, deserving or undeserving, civilized or uncivilized, among many other binaries (Takaki, 2023). Binary thinking also informs our understanding of resources and the distribution of resources among people. Although in most westernized countries, there are more than enough resources to distribute in an equitable way for people to have access to a healthy, thriving life, racialized capitalism, one form of a system of oppression, has resulted in the unequal distribution of resources (Davis, 2003). People with power have constructed capitalism in such a way that resources are distributed according to the perception of prestige associated with work, with some jobs paying more than others based on prestige of the position. As is not surprising in a system set up based on the exploitation of some people for the benefit of other people, wealthy, white, nondisabled, cisgender men benefit the most from this hierarchy, and people of color, feminized people, people with disabilities, and gender nonconforming people benefit the least and are most likely to be exploited. Further, wealth accumulation has little to do with work in modern day capitalism. People accumulate wealth based on their "ownership" of things including land and capital invested in business and other forms of economy. We have been socialized to consider resources, including money and other things considered capital, as finite, largely because of binary ways of thinking. This perspective about finite resources further contributes to individualistic, competitive and zero sum thinking.

When we view resources as finite, we see other people as competition rather than community members. Further, our zero-sum binary way of thinking results in individualistic thinking, especially about finite resources. When we see resources as finite, we engage in behavior that focuses on our individualistic access to those resources, focusing on getting more, more, more, rather than being in community with other people to ensure all people's well-being is achieved. Further, individualism results in deep socialization to think about what *I* can get from a situation, rather than what benefit something has for the collective. While this thinking informs our orientation to material resources and ownership, it is also closely related to our relationships to power, which is also constructed as a finite resource, meaning that we have been socialized to believe that if someone else gains access to power, that must somehow mean that we are losing it.

People living in a society in which power is treated as a limited resource, and where people must be "better" than others to be successful, results in a culture rooted in dominance and oppression. Systems of oppression perpetuate individualism, competition, and a zero-sum mentality. When we learn that we must dominate or be better than others to be successful, we internalize a problematic relationship to power. We enact power over other people to move ahead, resulting in all kinds of problematic relationships.

This competitive, zero-sum mentality is perpetuated almost everywhere we look. From a very early age, we teach children that to be "successful," they must do all the right things – go to the right college, interact with the right people, get the right degree, and get the right job. We teach kids that only some people get to have access to these "right" things (which is true – a limited number of people will be admitted to ivy league schools, for example), and that other people will never have access to them. Further, we insinuate that these are the *only* ways to be "right" and to be successful. The very nature of this kind of dominance sets up unhealthy relationships to power, and even more importantly, to other people. We teach kids to see their peers as competition rather than support. Everything is zero-sum – if I get this, you can't have it and vice versa. Not only does this competitive, individualistic mindset influence our relationship to power but also leads to dehumanization – for people with power to consider other people expendable or exploitable, they must see them as less than human and less than deserving.

Some harm and violence occur because people with privilege are socialized to believe that they are entitled to take whatever they want and they are taught to see some people as lesser than themselves, making it easier to cause harm. However, I *also* wonder how this socialization to entitlement also contributes to the harm of people with dominant identities.

Dehumanization, isolation, and disconnection. In many cases, people with incredible access to privilege and material wealth lack connection. A culture of dominance results in isolation for people with dominant identities (Raffo, 2022). When one is socialized to believe that everyone around them is their competition – someone they must beat to be successful – building authentic and meaningful relationships is difficult. Further, when expected to maintain dominance to be considered "successful," one must internalize the belief that they are better than others. This belief certainly results in dehumanizing other people, making it easier to cause harm to people one dehumanizes. However, it likely *also* contributes to people disconnecting from themselves, making it easier to harm other people (Raffo, 2022).

The relationship between trauma and supremacy is confusing. A result of trauma is disconnection, yet disconnection is also how "supremacy is socialized into bodies," making the relationship between trauma and supremacy a "mindfuck" (Raffo, 2022, p. 73). People socialized into dominant bodies have gained the ability to "retreat into a separated isolated self without actually feeling a sense of disconnection," and disconnection is *also* a result of trauma. She elaborates,

> *I deeply believe that raising babies to become white, male, or other dominant-culture adults who isolate in this way is a form of developmental trauma. It's an attachment disorder, a disconnection from unhealed generational wounds, all the way back to the original wounds on this land, which means a deep and generational form of disconnection. (pp. 68–69)*

Raffo (2022) continues, explaining that "dominance starts with a kind of developmental betrayal," but "supremacy then orders the world around itself" by using violence to ensure that people in dominant bodies maintain power and control (p. 69). Therefore, both trauma *and* dominance contribute to people enacting violence on other people.

Disconnection from self and others results in people lacking empathy and compassion for other people. Further, access to power contributes to lack of empathy and compassion. When people have access to significant amounts of power, they lose the ability to "mirror," which is the "basis of compassion" for most people (Raffo, 2022, p. 71). I have observed this in my relationships with even the kindest, most well-intended white men that I interact with. When someone shares with me a struggle or challenge they are managing, I often respond by saying, "I'm so sorry you're dealing with that." Recently, I have noticed that when I respond with "I'm sorry" to white men in my life they respond back with, "you don't need to be sorry." I engaged with one of them about this by saying, "I'm not sorry for anything I did – I'm simply empathizing with you." He responded in a joking manner, "Oh yeah, my wife keeps wanting me to have more of that[…]empathy." While he was joking, the point stands. Although he is a kind and loving human, he does not need empathy to survive his day-to-day life; in fact, his access to power may result in him cutting off his ability to empathize or feel what people around him feel. When one has access to power, they need not connect with other people for survival, nor understand or empathize with other people's experiences. Without compassion and empathy, some people may enact harm and violence on other people.

While entitlement and disconnection are two sides of the same coin when it comes to enacting harm and violence, they may require different interventions. Historically, we have primarily relied on addressing harm and violence from the entitlement side of the coin – trying to create more equitable environments and interrupt oppression so that people with power see people with minoritized identities as equals, and sometimes, simply even as humans who deserve the same level of respect as people with dominant identities. Certainly, one reason people engage in harmful behavior is because they see themselves as entitled to controlling other people and because they see other people as less than human, even subconsciously. This subconscious belief frequently comes from viewing people with minoritized identities as a threat to their "traditional" ways of being. When people's very existence threatens the dominant power structure in which cisgender, straight, white, wealthy, and nondisabled men hoard power, people with power may enact violence. Continuing to work toward eradication of oppression and creating environments in which all people share access to power is an essential part of violence prevention.

The other side of the coin, however, indicates that part of the reason that some people with power enact violence is because of their own intergenerational trauma and socialization into supremacy. This is harder for us to get our brains around. Given the high levels of privilege that people with dominant identities hold, it is sometimes difficult to have compassion for the trauma these individuals carry. Similarly, much of the disconnection enacted by people with incredible access to privilege is of their own creation, so why should the rest of us care? Certainly, it is not the responsibility of every person who has experienced violence to engage with and attempt to create spaces of healing for privileged people's trauma and disconnection. However, given that rates of violence, including sexual violence, are still very high, it may behoove at least some of us – especially those of us working on prevention efforts on college campuses – to consider working toward creating spaces where people with dominant identities can uncover and heal their wounds. Creating spaces rooted in accountability and healing may facilitate healing for people who have or may cause harm, which is another form of violence prevention.

IMPLICATIONS FOR SEXUAL VIOLENCE PREVENTION

Understanding the relationship between trauma, dominance, violence, and oppression can be challenging. Our orientation to seeing people as either "bad" or "good" results in us wanting to view people with considerable amounts of access to power as "bad," resulting in us not having compassion for people who engage in harmful behavior. While understanding the relationship between trauma, dominance, and violence does not *excuse* harmful behavior, it may help *explain* it, which may help us *address* it. If we approach people who engage in harmful behavior from a place of helping them heal from their own experiences with trauma and pain, we may make more progress toward eradicating violence than if we approach the work from a place of shaming them for their behaviors. As abolitionist thinkers remind us, no human is disposable, and we must work to engage people in their own healing to avoid causing future harm (Kaba & Ritchie, 2022). In the following sections, I describe the importance of creating spaces for healing and connection and creating developmentally focused programs for people who may or have caused harm (Henkle et al., 2020; Rapisarda et al., 2020).

Creating Spaces for Healing and Connection

We each have a responsibility to heal so we do not cause further harm to those around us. The roots of so much sexual violence are relational issues: lack of empathy and connection to other human beings contribute significantly to sexual violence among college students (Grimes, 2022; Hudson-Fledge et al., 2020). People engage in harmful sexual behavior when they lack empathy and understanding of others' experiences and seek to further establish their dominance and control, which are touted as signs of strength in an individualistic culture. People with incredible access to power and privilege often lack connection. Power and dominance thrive in individualistic cultures with a strong focus on strength and stoicism, the opposite of connection; therefore, an essential component of preventing violence is providing opportunities for people to develop authentic connections with each other.

In our current climate, creating opportunities for connection proves challenging because people are more divided on their perspectives and beliefs than ever before (Dimock & Wike, 2020). Engaging authentically with other people requires a certain level of vulnerability, and a willingness to not know all the answers. Engaging authentically to understand another person's perspective requires that people be willing to understand and learn from another person's perspective and consider changing their position on a topic or issue when they gain new information. Currently, our culture is so divided that being willing to change one's mind is seen as a sign of weakness. The very culture of dominance we seek to interrupt by providing space for people to reconnect to themselves and heal from intergenerational trauma upholds barriers for creating this space.

To create spaces of healing, I advocate for information and perspective sharing and trusted leaders modeling healing practices (Brown, 2021). Many healers write about their understanding of and experiences with the relationship between trauma and violence, including among people with dominant identities (e.g., Hassan, 2022; Page & Woodland, 2023; Raffo, 2022). For people who teach classes about human conditions, using these texts as a basis for exploring the level of harm and violence we see in our cultures may contribute to opportunities for students to better understand the connection between trauma and violence. If facilitated well, classrooms can be a nonthreatening space where students are exposed to new ideas and perspectives and encouraged to develop their own understanding of an issue or phenomenon (Brown, 2021). Similarly, for faculty and staff, book clubs and learning communities may facilitate a similar kind of opportunity for exposure to new ideas and discussions. Although power dynamics sometimes make book clubs and processing spaces difficult for some faculty and staff to participate in, developing spaces that consider various positionalities and power structures can alleviate some of these concerns.

Additionally, creating optional processing spaces for people to come together to share their perspectives, thoughts, and feelings about current issues is an opportunity for connection and healing (Brown, 2021). These spaces can be facilitated both by mental health clinicians and other healers in the community. Different people have different needs when it comes to healing spaces, and providing many different kinds of opportunities for healing and connection is important. Spaces for healing and connection often require some sort of previously existing relationship for people to feel comfortable participating; therefore, starting with already established communities may be an important strategy for these spaces. For example, a few years ago, after a semester with significant instances of violence and harm that impacted many staff members' well-being, we offered two different kinds of sessions for people from a variety of perspectives. First, we engaged in an open processing space with just members of our center's advisory board. We invited people who wanted to come and be present with one another, listening to, sharing, and being in community with each other, bearing witness to each other's pain. A few weeks later, we invited a mental health counselor from off-campus to come and facilitate sessions for people engaged at different levels of the organization. He facilitated three different sessions to allow for people at different levels to participate without their supervisors in the same space. Staff responded positively to each of these spaces, and we must find ways to develop these in on-going ways.

This example focuses on staff, but similar communities for healing and connection could focus on student groups and organizations. In fact, many student groups and organizations include belonging, connection, and engagement as part of their purpose and mission, so supporting students to fulfill this part of their mission and explicitly tying it to healing and connection could be a strategy. Ultimately, opportunities for healing and connection could stretch across the campus to faculty, staff, *and* students. Creating a culture in which community members prioritize healing and connection is no small task. Given how dominant culture prioritizes strength, stoicism, individualism, and disconnection as markers of success, introducing and connecting well-being and mental health as priorities will take time and patience.

Approach People Who Cause Harm With Accountability *and* Healing

Given our long history of approaching people who engage in harmful behavior, especially sexual violence, from a strictly punitive place, developing strategies to hold people who cause harm accountable *and* supporting them in their own healing is no small task. Through the interpretation of federal guidance related to adjudicating sexual misconduct (examined more in Chapter 4), many campuses have begun to implement respondent services on their campuses (Henkle et al., 2020; Rapisarda et al., 2020). These services largely came about as a result of respondents claiming that institutions did not provide due process for respondents (Henkle et al., 2020; Wilgus & Lowery, 2018), resulting in the interpretation of the services being "equal to" or the "the same" as victim advocacy. As is often the case, while I disagree with how we got here, I am an advocate for respondent services. I do, however, believe there is a major difference between "respondent services" and "victim advocacy." Given higher education policymakers' desire to simplify things, this nuance has been lost in the guidance (Henkle et al., 2020), making many people resistant to providing respondent services because it feels like we are advocating that people who cause harm should not be held accountable. In fact, respondent services programs, if designed correctly, could both engage people who engaged in harmful behavior in a process of accountability *and* healing at the same time (Rapisarda et al., 2020). Unfortunately, in our adversarial, court-like processes, sexual misconduct adjudication processes quickly turn into legal – rather than developmental – processes (Collins, 2016; Roskin-Frazee, 2023; Wilgus & Tabachnick, 2020). When sexual misconduct cases moved from student conduct offices, where staff were trained in student development and learning, to Title IX offices, where staff are primarily trained in the legal and compliance aspect of adjudication, many opportunities for learning and development have been lost (Anderson, 2016).

As discussed earlier in the chapter, the overlap between "victim" and "perpetrator" is significant – albeit, not always in the same case (though this is also true sometimes). Given that a significant number of people who engage in harmful sexual behavior have also experienced harmful sexual behavior (Gámez-Guadix et al., 2011), it is important for prevention efforts to provide healing for people who have both experienced and caused harm.

As explored in more detail in Chapter 4, accountability is significantly more work for the person who engaged in harmful behavior than the person who experienced the harmful behavior, while punishment is the opposite. Usually, systems designed to punish people for wrong-doing end up putting more labor on the person who experienced the harm than on the person who caused the harm. The person who experienced harm is responsible for "proving" that they experienced harm and must tell their story over and over to prove their case. *If* the case does result in the person who caused harm being held responsible, punishment in a punitive process is passive – the person who caused harm is simply acted upon rather than taking responsibility and engaging in accountability for their actions (Sered, 2019). In a system that focuses on accountability over punishment, the person who engaged in harmful behavior takes responsibility for the harm and seeks to repair the harm caused, which requires action and engagement on the part of the person who caused harm.

Not only can accountability be more healing than punitive responses for the person who experienced harm but it also requires active engagement by the person who caused harm, resulting in them being less likely to cause harm in the future (Sered, 2019). Rather than resisting respondent services, we could focus on creating respondent services with an educational and developmental focus, helping people who engaged in harmful behavior to better understand how their behavior impacts those around them.

CONCLUSION

Engaging with people who cause harm can sometimes feel counterintuitive in our culture focused on carceral responses to violence. However, survivors – especially survivors with minoritized identities – call on us to develop noncarceral responses to sexual violence (Decker et al., 2022; Dixon & Piepzna-Samarasinha, 2020; Gartner et al., 2024; Sered, 2019). Further, given that carceral responses to violence have not resulted in a reduction in violence (Muehlenhard et al., 2017; Sered, 2019), to eradicate sexual violence on our campuses and beyond, we must consider new approaches. Engaging with people who cause harm to heal from their own experiences with violence and trauma may contribute an additional piece of the puzzle to finally end sexual violence. In the following chapter, I return to the awareness–prevention–response trifecta to illustrate the strategies campus leaders currently engage to address sexual violence.

3

AWARENESS OF SEXUAL VIOLENCE AMONG COLLEGE STUDENTS

ABSTRACT

In this chapter, I provide a brief history of campus sexual violence awareness-raising on college campuses, followed by an analysis of a few current awareness-raising strategies. I examine social media, poster campaigns, and awareness months, as well as prevalence, consequences, and resources related to the awareness ring of the prevention, response, and awareness trifecta. I problematize best practices and advocate for campuses to spend fewer resources on awareness and more resources on prevention.

Keywords: Sexual violence; awareness; education; best practices; campaigns

As described in Chapter 1, many campus administrators and educators engage in strategies focused on awareness, response, and prevention to address sexual violence among college students. The *awareness* part of the trifecta refers to the ways in which scholars, educators, and activists attempt to bring the problem of sexual violence into the consciousness of key stakeholders. Although there is overlap between awareness and prevention in the form of education, activists, scholars, and educators often conflate awareness and prevention. Raising awareness about sexual violence is certainly an important piece of the puzzle; however, in and of itself, awareness does not prevent sexual violence.

A common challenge that educators must navigate is the reality that students all come with different starting points in their understanding of sexual violence. Often, awareness-related programming focuses on letting people know that there is a problem with sexual violence and the consequences of violence for victims (Kettrey et al., 2023). Many students are starting to push back on this kind of awareness programming. They describe the programming as condescending, unhelpful, and ineffective (Chugani et al., 2021; Karunaratne & Harris, 2022; Worthen & Wallace, 2021). Many college students report that they are highly aware that sexual violence and its consequences are problems; rather, the lack of awareness comes from understanding what constitutes sexual violence and harm, especially on the part of the person causing harm (Worthen & Wallace, 2021).

Raising awareness about sexual violence is crucial for eradicating it. When people do not understand the significance of a problem, they cannot work to address it. However, people must have accurate and complete information to effectively address sexual violence, which requires activists, scholars, and educators to operate from a power-conscious perspective. In this chapter, I provide a brief history of campus sexual violence awareness-raising on college campuses, followed by an analysis of a few current awareness-raising strategies. Finally, I explore some of the challenges of the content typically used in awareness-raising education.

HISTORICAL PERSPECTIVES

Although people, and even more specifically women of color, have been organizing around issues of sexual violence for centuries (Giddings, 1984; Greensite, 2009; McGuire, 2010), many scholars identify the 1970s and 1980s as a significant turning point for addressing sexual violence on college campuses (Bevacqua, 2000; Bohmer & Parrot, 1993; Corrigan, 2013). During this time, activists worked to raise awareness about the problem of sexual violence on college campuses, interrupting myths about sexual violence and helping people understand the nature of sexual violence. In the 1970s, feminists initiated and engaged in a variety of consciousness-raising groups, working to support women in coming to understand the ways they experience sexism. In addition to addressing sexism and sexual harassment in the workplace, reproductive justice issues, and political and cultural power of women, feminists also continued to raise awareness about interpersonal violence, including sexual violence (Bevacqua, 2000). Activists in the 1970s through the 1990s also engaged in a variety of activist campaigns designed to raise awareness about sexual assault, including marches, protests, and demonstrations, some of which still exist in some form today (Bevacqua, 2000). For example, Take Back the Night, The Clothesline Project, and Vagina Monologues are examples of longstanding awareness-raising events related to sexual violence. In 2006, Aishah Shahidah Simmons released the film, *NO! The Rape Documentary*, reminding viewers about the unique relationship between racism, sexism, and sexual violence for Black women (NO! The rape documentary, n.d.). Each of these events contributes to the ongoing discussion related to sexual violence on college and university campuses today.

Part of the awareness-raising related to sexual violence in the 1970s and 1980s was identifying the insidiousness of acquaintance sexual violence, which, at the time, was referred to as "date rape" (Koss, 1985; Warshaw, 1988). A breakthrough study in 1987 illuminated the problem of sexual violence in acquaintance or dating situations among college students. Koss and colleagues surveyed more than 6,000 students on 32 campuses, highlighting the reality that one in four college women experienced a completed or attempted sexual assault during her college career (Koss et al., 1987). This work paved the way for activists and educators to raise awareness about sexual violence as a significant problem beyond that of stranger rape. In consultation with the Ms. Foundation for Education, Robin Warshaw (1988) advanced Koss's work through the groundbreaking book, *I Never Called It Rape*, which illuminated and gave language to the experiences of thousands of college women as it related to sexual violence. Although many feminists and activists already knew that they had been experiencing rape and sexual violence in dating relationships, Koss and Warshaw helped to validate their experiences, giving language to their experiences and legitimizing it through research. Unfortunately, this early research failed to account for identities and experiences with oppression beyond that of gender and sexism, leading to limited information about the ways that racism, classism, ableism, and homophobia also influence people's experiences with sexual violence.

STRATEGIES AND CONTENT

Today, activists and educators build on this history to raise awareness about sexual violence on college campuses. Activists employ a variety of strategies and organize many events to raise people's awareness about sexual violence. In this chapter, I examine strategies (i.e., social media, poster campaigns, and awareness months) and content (i.e., prevalence, consequences, and resources) related to the awareness ring of the prevention, response, and awareness trifecta.

Strategies

Activists and educators use a variety of methods to attempt to raise awareness about sexual violence among college students. Over the past several years, social media has expanded as a strategy for reaching people as it relates to raising awareness about sexual violence among college students (Hosie, 2020; Nicolla et al., 2023). Educators and activists have used Tik Tok, X, and Instagram as outlets for raising awareness about sexual violence. By now, one of the #MeToo movements is ubiquitous as an example of awareness raising on social media (Boyd & McEwan, 2024). Although Tarana Burke used the phrase "me too" to illuminate the problem of childhood sexual abuse as early as 2006 (Burke, 2021), the term became a hashtag in 2017, igniting a viral movement of women sharing their stories as survivors of sexual harassment and sexual assault (Boyd & McEwan, 2024). Certainly, many people have critiqued the #MeToo movement for coopting a Black woman's work related to sexual violence (Boyd & McEwan, 2024), and yet, the impact of the hashtag movement starting in 2017 cannot be overstated. For a while, everywhere I turned – research articles, newspaper articles and blog posts – referred to the #MeToo movement in its opening lines. While I highly doubt that the #MeToo movement *prevented* any sexual assaults from happening, it did shed light on the on-going reality of the prevalence of sexual violence and opened the doors for some survivors to share their stories with friends, family, and strangers in ways that they had not before. The sheer number of people sharing their stories illustrated the power of community and likely contributed to increased healing for some survivors of sexual violence.

In fact, some survivors report that awareness and education related to sexual violence contribute to their healing from their own experiences of violence (Harris et al., 2021; Karunaratne, 2023). Social media posts explaining the dynamics and consequences of sexual violence help some survivors feel less isolated and helped them understand their experiences as legitimate and valid despite other messages that their experiences were not "bad" enough to be considered "violent" (Karunaratne, 2023).

One of the benefits of social media as a mechanism to raise awareness about sexual violence is that some of the awareness raising happens organically rather than being organized by sexual violence educators. This organic awareness-raising may contribute to people learning new things without being educated in formal settings, which may reduce their defensiveness to the messages (Nicolla et al., 2023). TikTok, a highly used social media platform, presents an interesting place to examine messages related to sexual violence. Certainly, after some time, some educators intentionally used TikTok as a tool to reach students, yet some of the beauty of TikTok is the way that everyday people, and many of them young people, used TikTok to express their own perspectives and experiences about social justice-related issues, raising people's awareness and consciousness while simply scrolling through their TikTok feeds (Mendes et al., 2019).

While the organic nature of personal experiences shared on social media certainly has some benefits, especially in the form of reaching new or different audiences, there are also some drawbacks. Social media works based on algorithms that influence what appears in our feeds. Algorithms are based on our previous likes and interests, which can contribute to the echo chamber nature of social media, where we tend to be exposed to things in our feeds that reiterate what we already believe or think, rather than exposing us to new ideas or perspectives (Benjamin, 2019). Similarly, some information shared on social media may be inaccurate, contributing to myths and misperceptions related to sexual violence (Nicolla & Lazard, 2023).

Some awareness-related strategies include creating posters to correct people's misperceptions about a problem or issue (Hills & Adams, 2023). Largely rooted in social norming philosophies, the purpose of many poster campaigns is to interrupt myths about sexual violence or to make people think differently about a problem (Potter & Stapleton, 2012). Poster campaigns often focus on grabbing people's attention through provocative statements or visually appealing graphics to make people pause and think. While traditional posters hung on bulletin boards throughout campuses are still common, technology has also allowed us to expand these campaigns beyond paper posters hung around campuses. Today, some campaigns use posters on digital campus boards that continually scroll, allowing multiple messages to be shared simultaneously (Hills & Adams, 2023). Similarly, some campaigns use Instagram to share the same posters shared on digital and physical bulletin boards, reiterating the message in multiple places.

Finally, one major strategy for raising awareness about sexual violence is Sexual Assault Awareness Month (SAAM), which is in April in the US (Pecoraro, n.d.). The coordination of many events across many entities during a concentrated period of time may assist in the density of the messaging, helping to keep a focus on the problem of sexual violence front and center for a period of time. SAAM events focus on prevalence of violence, consequences of violence for survivors, and creating spaces of healing for survivors, all of which are crucial elements of raising awareness of a problem and creating community for survival and healing. That said, one of the drawbacks to awareness months is that they sometimes perpetuate surface-level awareness-raising and allow people to participate in one-time, feel-good programming without engaging in the depth necessary to truly understand and address the problem of sexual violence.

For example, some popular programs that take place during SAAM include Red Flag campaigns and signing pledges. While each of these programs may be an important start to a conversation about the nuance and dynamics of violence, they too often consume major resources including staff time and money, with little known benefit. Awareness month events typically reach the students already invested in the issue rather than reaching new students who may not otherwise hear the message. Similarly, these activities that have gained traction as "best practices" for SAAM may contribute to unintentionally placing responsibility on those targeted for harm to end violence. For example, Red Flag campaigns typically focus on red flags in relationships that one should avoid or leave a situation if the behavior occurs. While creating space for people to talk about healthy and unhealthy behaviors in relationships is important, it is also important to focus on telling people not to engage in the behavior rather than *only* focusing on teaching people to avoid or leave a situation where someone engages in the behavior. Red flag campaigns focused on teaching those at risk for experiencing harm without also educating those who have potential to cause the harm only provide opportunities for individual people to avoid harm, rather than stopping the harm from happening in the first place.

Similarly, signing pledges to believe survivors, to stop violence from happening around you or to not engage in violent behaviors yourself only go so far without deep and nuanced conversations about harm. Certainly, most people will sign a pledge that says they will do these things – no one openly admits to disbelieving survivors, allowing violence to happen around them, or enacting violence themselves. Although identifying harm and violence should be straightforward for people, it is not. People have varying levels of what is acceptable for them, and our heightened focus on criminality and policy related to violence results in a hyperfocus on what is illegal rather than what is harmful to another person. Further, pledge signing may result in increased likelihood for harm. Some people who engage in harmful behavior do so under the guise of protection or use their status as a "feminist" to get close to a target to cause them harm (Armato, 2013; Linder & Johnson, 2015).

While certainly, awareness months are a starting place to engage people in nuanced conversations about sexual violence, they are far too often the end point of engagement for many individuals. While not the fault of the people organizing awareness months, the reality is that most awareness months cycle through events named as "best practices" by professional organizations or groups rather than events that may reach students on a particular campus. Further, given the organizational structure of most campuses, finding resources and support for engaging in nuanced, in-depth education about sexual violence is difficult. Educators are expected to create SAAM events because it has been determined a "best practice" and is a way for administrators to tally their work addressing violence. Counting the number of events hosted and the people who attend the events is far easier than examining the actual change that could happen as a result of more intense, yet less well-attended, community-specific, nuanced conversation. Awareness is a start, yet that start so often becomes the finish line, given the competing interests and many awareness months present on a university calendar.

We move from Black history month to women's history month then to SAAM without often recognizing the deep interconnections between the three (among many others).

In addition to considering the strategies people might employ for raising awareness about sexual violence, it is also important to examine the content of awareness-related strategies, highlighting a need for accuracy in information.

Content

Given that raising awareness about an issue is often a foray into a topic for people, it is important to keep the information straightforward and simple. However, given that sexual violence is anything but straightforward and simple, it is difficult to figure out ways to provide accurate information in simple terms, allowing people to gain insight into a nuanced problem.

As described above, one of the significant aspects of the history of sexual violence awareness-raising includes making people aware of the prevalence and type of sexual violence happening on college campuses. Today, the message that one in four women will experience sexual violence in her college career is prevalent and students report a high level of awareness about sexual violence (Cantor et al., 2019). Activists and educators share the prevalence message through educational programs, including orientation and mandatory online training for new college students. Further, reporters frequently focus on this statistic when reporting about sexual violence in written and television media (Baumgartner & McAdon, 2017; McCummings et al., 2018). In fact, one organization to address sexual violence by engaging men as active bystanders is even called "One in Four" ("One in Four," n.d.).

Despite the increased awareness of the prevalence of sexual violence on college campuses, some challenges exist. One of the challenges associated with the understanding of the prevalence of campus sexual violence is that without nuanced discussion, this straightforward and simple messaging may unintentionally center white women, perpetuate stranger danger myths, and make people who cause harm invisible.

Centering White Women

Because research frequently fails to disaggregate data based on identities other than a binary gender, the one in four statistic about campus sexual assault primarily applies to heterosexual, white, and cisgender women (Muehlenhard et al., 2017). Most research on campus sexual violence includes an over-representation of white women and rarely includes demographic information on sexual orientation, ability or gender identity (Harris et al., 2020; Linder et al., 2020). The few studies that have disaggregated data based on identities including race, ability, sexual orientation, and gender identity illuminate that people who cause harm often target people with minoritized identities at higher rates than their dominant group peers (Cantor et al., 2019). However, dominant narratives still prioritize cisgender heterosexual white women at large colleges and universities through media and other representations (Harris, 2020; Wooten, 2017).

The implications of focusing on only one type of victim in campus sexual violence education are significant. When people are taught to picture a pretty, white, cisgender, straight woman as the primary victim of sexual violence, they likely fail to consider other people as potential victims. Failing to consider that other people may also be victims of sexual violence means that well-meaning students, educators, and administrators likely unintentionally minimize some students' experiences with sexual violence, resulting in them not receiving the care they need (Harris et al., 2021; Zounlome et al., 2019). For example, when a gay man student discloses to an academic advisor that he wants to drop a class because he is struggling with what he describes as a "personal issue" with someone in the class, it is unlikely the academic advisor would think of sexual violence as the potential "personal issue" unless the advisor had power-conscious education (or personal experience) related to sexual violence. Given that victims are portrayed as white, cisgender, heterosexual women, the academic advisor may consider sexual violence as a potential issue if a white, cisgender, and heterosexual woman presents this problem to them but not in the case of a gay male student. The academic advisor may not think to offer resources related to interpersonal violence to the male student and he may miss out on potential resources that could serve him.

Similarly, if people primarily picture white cisgender women as victims of sexual violence, they may not see women of color as targets of harm, resulting in women of color minimizing their own experiences with harm and people providing support services also minimizing those experiences (Zounlome et al., 2019). In fact, Black women, frequently portrayed as "strong," may not feel comfortable seeking services from a victim advocacy program, nor even consider their experience worthy of attention (West et al., 2016). Similarly, research indicates that white women do not see Black women as potential victims in bystander intervention scenarios (Katz et al., 2017). Centering white women in sexual violence awareness programming results in other students not receiving the attention they deserve and contributes to the ineffectiveness of awareness programming overall.

Invisibility and Misperceptions of People Who Cause Harm

Similar to the ways that statistics may contribute to misperceptions about who victims of sexual violence are, these same statistics contribute to making some people who cause harm invisible and others hypervisible (Patton & Snyder-Yuly, 2007; Zounlome et al., 2021). The one in four statistic fails to name and address people who cause harm, which subliminally contributes to placing disproportionate responsibility on victims to prevent sexual violence. Focusing only on victims in media coverage and research may result in people who cause harm, especially white, middle-class perpetrators, remaining invisible. The ways activists, scholars, and journalists report statistics portray sexual assault as something that just happens, and no one is responsible for committing it (Wesley et al., 2022). What if instead of focusing exclusively on victims of sexual violence, the statistics *also* focused on the number of people who caused harm? For example, by stating, "One in seven college men have committed acts of sexual violence" (Gidycz et al., 2011) rather than "One in four women will experience sexual violence in college," people may have a different understanding of who causes harm. What if scholars, activists, and journalists spent as much time and energy on statistics about people who cause harm as they do on the statistic about one in four women experiencing sexual violence? What if college students could specifically name that one in seven men has committed an act of sexual violence? How would this shift the responsibility and focus of sexual violence prevention?

Similar to the research about victimization, most participants in studies about perpetration include white, middle-class, heterosexual, and assumingly cisgender men (Linder et al., 2020). Although the participants of these studies include primarily white, heterosexual, and cisgender men, researchers frequently fail to name the racial identities of their participants. If a study had over 80% Black or African American participants, researchers would most certainly describe the racial identity of their participants and likely attribute many of their findings to race; however, because whiteness is invisible and considered the norm in mainstream western society, researchers fail to name the relationship between whiteness and perpetration that likely exists. Working from the tenet of the power-conscious framework to name and interrupt dominant group members' investment in and benefit from systems of oppression, scholars and activists must do more to name perpetrators' responsibility for sexual violence.

At the same time, white men are invisible as people who cause harm whereas men of color (and in particular Black and Latino men) are hypervisible as people who cause harm. Media representations of sexual assault frequently include photos of men of color who have engaged in harmful behavior but not white men (Colburn & Melander, 2018). Similarly, authors of timely warning alerts sent on college campus overuse racial identifiers when the suspect of a crime is a man of color and underutilize racial identifiers when the suspect is white (Pelfrey et al., 2018; Sherman, 2022). Without intervention to correct these misperceptions, "best practices" for raising awareness perpetuate harmful racist myths about both victims and people engaged in harmful behavior.

Stranger Danger Myths

Despite knowing that sexual violence happens at alarming rates on college campuses, many students still subscribe to stranger danger myths, meaning that they believe that most sexual assault is committed by strangers rather than people known to the victims (Fisher & Sloan, 2003; Hayes-Smith & Levett, 2010). Although students may be aware of the high rates of sexual violence on college campuses, their strategies for protecting themselves still revolve around stranger danger myths. In a study conducted at a southeastern university in the US, cisgender women students identified carrying pepper spray and other weapons, not walking alone at night, and watching their drinks at parties and bars as their primary strategies for reducing their risk of sexual violence (Linder & Lacy, 2019). Further, most campus safety websites offer tips for preventing sexual assault and many of these tips focus on victims' responsibility to prevent sexual assault and focus on stranger danger. These safety tips primarily focus on women as targets for violence and men as the people targeting them (Bedera & Nordmeyer, 2015; Lund & Thomas, 2015). Although it is important for people to be cognizant of their safety in a variety of settings, it is also important for people to recognize that they are more likely to be targeted by someone they know than by someone they do not know. In fact, 86% of sexual assaults happen when a person targets someone they know for violence (Black et al., 2011).

Further, most sexual violence happens between people of similar socioeconomic classes and happens intraracially (between people of the same race; Black et al., 2011). Except for Native American women, most people are assaulted by people of the same race. Given the history of colonization and current context of ineffective legal strategies for addressing violence perpetrated by non-Native people on Native American reservations, Native American women are often targeted by white perpetrators (Deer, 2015, 2017). Despite this history, most white women are socialized to fear the "other," specifically Black and Latino men who are strangers to them. Media representations of people who engage in sexual violence contribute to this narrative about people who cause harm, resulting in people misperceiving who people who engage in sexual violence are (Meyers, 2004; Patton & Snyder-Yuly, 2007).

The misunderstanding of the dynamics of sexual violence may contribute to an increased risk of sexual violence because students fail to understand the appropriate times to intervene and "protect" themselves from the wrong people. Although it is never a potential victim's responsibility to protect themselves from sexual assault, people – especially women and gender nonbinary people – do engage in a fair number of strategies to reduce their risk of being targeted for sexual assault. However, because people misperceive and misunderstand the dynamics of sexual violence, they are usually not protecting themselves from the people most likely to cause harm – people they know, trust, and are in relationship with. Teaching students to understand the nuanced dynamics of sexual violence may contribute to a reduced risk of violence. When students understand that people they know are more likely to target them as potential targets of sexual assault, they may be more astute to some warning signs that people who cause harm display.

CONCLUSION

Although women of color have organized for centuries around addressing sexual violence at the intersection of racism and sexism (McGuire, 2010), many campus activists primarily focus on sexism as the root of sexual violence. Some activists strive to address racism, homophobia, transphobia, and additional forms of oppression in their organizing, but when relying on limited historical perspectives and power-neutral research, nuance related to other forms of oppression often gets lost. Raising awareness about campus sexual violence through a power-conscious lens remains important in a climate where more and more people are invested in addressing campus sexual assault. Failing to account for the ways in which identities and power influence people's understanding of sexual violence results in less than effective strategies for preventing and eventually eradicating sexual violence. In the next chapter, I will examine response to campus sexual violence, highlighting current campus practices and advocating for more power-conscious approaches to effectively responding to sexual violence on college and university campuses.

4

RESPONDING TO SEXUAL VIOLENCE AMONG COLLEGE STUDENTS

ABSTRACT

In this chapter, I describe the influence of carceral practices on campus sexual misconduct adjudication processes. I illustrate the connections between the criminal punishment systems and campus adjudication processes, with a specific focus on racism oppression. I describe the difference between accountability and punishment, illustrating that criminal punishment systems and sexual misconduct adjudication processes do not allow for accountability, nor healing for any parties involved. A heavy focus on compliance results in administrators prioritizing risk management over prevention of sexual violence.

Keywords: Carcerality; criminal punishment systems; campus sexual misconduct adjudication; response to sexual violence; accountability

The *response* ring of the awareness–response–prevention trifecta refers to the ways educators and administrators address sexual violence after it happens, including punishment and accountability processes and healing for survivors. Given the current climate of increased legislation and litigation and student activism related to campus sexual violence, administrators frequently have no choice but to spend significant resources on campus violence response (Linder, Karunaratne, & Grimes, 2024; Méndez, 2020; Silbaugh, 2015). In fact, most policy related to sexual violence incentivizes responding to sexual assault over engaging in activities to prevent sexual assault from happening in the first place. As Silbaugh (2015) astutely notes,

> *Title IX strongly incentivizes the post-assault focus. Colleges may want to reduce the overall rate of sexual assault, but they risk liability under Title IX primarily for a bad response to an assault that has already occurred, rather than for ineffective efforts to reduce the overall rate of assault. (p. 1052)*

Not only are campus administrators required to spend significant resources responding to sexual violence after it happens, most of these responses fail to eradicate sexual violence. Similar to other systems rooted in punishment and carcerality, campus response systems focus on individualized responses to violence and do not end violence but rather move violence to happening somewhere else (Kaba & Ritchie, 2022). Additionally, the litigious society in which we exist results in interpretation of campus policies being more focused on complying with the law to avoid "getting in trouble" than to prevent future violence (Silbaugh, 2015). While many people place responsibility for this culture of compliance on university administrators, I argue that they are only part of the problem – the reality is that policymakers constructed laws and policies requiring a focus on complying with a law, rather than really understanding the intention behind the law and to eradicate violence.

As described in the Introduction, since writing the first edition of this book, I have become more immersed in understanding the influence of carcerality on response systems, including those dedicated to addressing sexual violence among college students. Further, I have come to a different understanding of punishment and accountability than I had when I wrote the first edition of this book. To that end, I start this chapter with a brief history of the criminal punishment system in the US, including its connections to carcerality, accountability, and punishment. I then move to reviewing campus policy, campus adjudication processes, and survivor support services through a lens of carcerality.

THE HISTORIES OF CRIMINAL PUNISHMENT SYSTEMS

Although most people have been socialized to see policing and other aspects of the criminal punishment system as neutral and fair, this is far from the truth. People with power designed criminal punishment systems to maintain power and dominance at the expense of people with minoritized identities (Kaba & Ritchie, 2022; Vitale, 2017). As it relates to sexual violence, the criminal punishment system has caused significant harm to survivors of sexual violence, especially Black and Indigenous survivors, and has failed to eradicate or even lessen sexual violence (Goodmark, 2023; Kaba & Ritchie, 2022).

As European colonizers worked to organize early legal systems in what is now considered the US, they focused on the issues of wealthy white men who were the only people who could access legal systems. With regard to sexual violence, this meant that men were the only people who could make a claim of sexual violence, and the crime was considered a property crime because white men's property – typically their daughter or wife – had been harmed (Freedman, 2013). The law distinguished between "rape" and "seduction." A charge of rape required "carnal knowledge," which typically meant physical violence and evidence of physical violence. Seduction laws focused on men coercing women into sex, resulting in a woman then being required to marry the man because they were no longer "pure." In fact, the consequences if a man was found guilty of "seduction" was frequently to marry the woman he seduced (Freedman, 2013). Women were literally forced to marry the person who caused harm to them and had no agency to pursue legal proceedings on their own. Because the crime was a property crime and men were the only people who could hold property, only men could file charges related to seduction (Freedman, 2013).

In addition to the sexist interpretation of the law, enactors of the new criminal punishment system also perpetrated racism. Specifically, people interpreting and enacting the law did not consider the rape of non-white women a crime and frequently punished Black men for rape even when they did not commit it (McGuire, 2010). White men raped enslaved women and Indigenous women at extremely high rates as a form of economic exploitation and terrorization to control them. Because the children of enslaved women became the property of the slave owner, the owner frequently raped enslaved women as way to increase their labor supply and therefore economic power (Freedman, 2013; McGuire, 2010). Further, colonizers used rape as a tool of terrorization directed at Indigenous communities, which continues to this day. Native American women experience higher rates of sexual violence than any other racial group and are the only group of women who experience higher rates of interracial, rather than intraracial, rape (Deer, 2015, 2017). Despite these experiences, Black and Indigenous women could not access the criminal punishment system because it was set up to serve white, owning-class people.

After slavery legally ended in the mid-1800s in the US, white men continued to rape Black women to exert power and control. Although formerly enslaved people were technically no longer "property," they still could not access the criminal punishment system, so white men were never charged or punished for raping Black and Indigenous women (Donat & D'Emilio, 1992; McGuire, 2010). Further, as formerly enslaved people began to gain greater access to power through owning businesses, white men used rape as one of their many tools of terrorization and control. When white men looted Black-owned businesses, they also raped Black women to further illustrate the level of control they still maintained. Although Black communities resisted and persevered, they did so without the support of legal systems (McGuire, 2010).

At the same time white men raped Black women with impunity, Black men were being punished through formal legal systems and through lynch mobs. Because white men considered white women the ultimate symbol of purity in mainstream US culture, white men forbade white women's engagement with Black men postemancipation (Freedman, 2013). White communities frequently mobbed and lynched Black men for merely interacting with white women, even in situations where white women consented and engaged in relationships with Black men. This lynching took place in public settings and without formal engagement of the criminal punishment system though police officers were frequently involved as instigators of the lynchings. Further, most of these lynchings of Black men happened at the same time as white men were raping Black women who had little recourse (Freedman, 2013; Giddings, 1984).

The US legal system is especially damaging to Indigenous women who live on tribal lands as it relates to rape and sexual violence. European colonizers used rape as a tool of colonization and terrorization during the founding of North America, and this legacy of colonization and violence continues today (Deer, 2015). People living on tribal lands have sovereignty from the US government, meaning that they can set up their own legal processes rather than participating in the mainstream US criminal punishment system (Deer, 2017). However, nontribal members cannot be prosecuted in a tribal court. Given that Indigenous women experience exceptionally high rates of sexual violence by white men, this results in white men escaping punishment for their criminal actions on tribal lands. Although Congress passed the Major Crimes Act in 1885 to claim jurisdiction over felony crimes on tribal lands, the law is rarely enforced and federal prosecutors rarely take on cases of sexual violence on tribal lands despite Indigenous people's plea that they do (Deer, 2017). Reports from 2009 through 2015 indicate that most of the cases that federal prosecutors declined to pursue on tribal lands included physical or sexual assaults, sexual exploitation or failure to register as a sex offender. Between 2005 and 2009, federal prosecutors declined to prosecute 67% of cases related to sexual violence on tribal lands (Deer, 2017).

CARCERALITY, ACCOUNTABILITY, AND PUNISHMENT

Not only does the criminal punishment system explicitly perpetuate racism and classism, it also relies on carcerality to maintain white supremacy and dominance. Although at first glance, the concept of carcerality seems to refer to the use of prisons and policing to control people, a deeper dive illustrates that carcerality exists beyond police and prisons. Carcerality refers to systems of punishment, surveillance, and control to maintain dominance, often disguised as "safety" (Kaba & Ritchie, 2022). People with power claim that they are making societies safer by maintaining the status quo, but as illustrated below criminal punishment systems actually increase, rather than decrease, violence. Invoked in most practices claiming to address sexual violence, carcerality influences our work on college campuses as much as it does the larger culture of responding to violence (Collins, 2016). The primary function of carcerality is control, which manifests in ensuring that dominant groups maintain their comfort, usually at the expense of minoritized groups (Linder, Karunaratne, et al., 2024).

Punishment is a central component of carcerality, stemming from the belief that people engage in harmful behavior because they are "bad" people. Carceral systems that enact punishment on people who engage in illegal behaviors only exacerbate harm rather than end it (Kaba & Ritchie, 2022; Sered, 2019). As Danielle Sered of Common Justice (2020) highlights, criminal punishment systems are criminogenic, resulting in increased violence by people engaged in criminal punishment systems. She describes the reality that people engage in violence primarily because of four things: shame, isolation, exposure to violence, and an inability to meet one's economic needs. She describes prisons as reiterating these very four things, resulting in an increase, rather than decrease, in violence (Common Justice, 2020).

Although we frequently use terms like consequences, punishment, justice, and accountability interchangeably, they are not interchangeable concepts. Carcerality focuses on controlling people through punishment for bad behavior rather than understanding the behavior and correcting it (Kaba & Ritchie, 2022). Instead of engaging people who have caused harm or violence in healing and repair, carcerality attempts to remove them from society to alleviate our collective responsibility for addressing harm at all levels (Sered, 2019). Additionally, carceral and punitive responses do not provide healing for survivors (Decker et al., 2022; Sered, 2019). Healing for both victims and people who cause harm should be a central goal of any system or process responding to acts of harm or violence. Unfortunately, our current systems and practices – on college campuses and beyond – do not contribute to anyone's healing.

Understanding the difference between accountability and punishment helps to illustrate the challenges with punitive processes as causing further harm rather than providing opportunities for healing for either victims or people who cause harm. Accountability is active and punishment is passive (Sered, 2019). Accountability requires the person who engaged in harmful behavior to take responsibility for the behavior and address it. Punishment does not require either of these things. The table below illustrates the active and passive elements of punishment and accountability.

Accountability	Punishment
Something one chooses to do	Is imposed by others with power over them (e.g., "the state")
Recognizes and requires a person's power, including their power to enact repair	Aims to diminish or contain a person's power, which it assumes can only be harmful
Is active: Requires a person to address suffering they caused by seeking to transform themselves and to mend and rebuild for others	Is passive: Requires a person to address suffering they caused only by suffering themselves with no pathway to provide anything to others
Deepens relationship and connection	Severs relationship and connection
Fosters healing and restoration	Fosters shame and isolation

Accountability processes likely create *less* work for the person who experienced the harm, while punishment creates *more* work for the person who experienced harm. Because in our criminal punishment systems it is the state's responsibility to "prove" that the person who caused harm did so, it often requires that the person who experienced harm relive their experience over and over in many venues to attempt to have people believe them. With accountability, there is no need for proof – the person who caused harm can take accountability for that harm *without fear of punishment*. They can seek to understand how they caused harm, where that harm came from inside them, and what they need to do to correct it. Further, they can listen to the person that they harmed to learn how to rectify that harm, contributing to both parties' healing.

Rarely do survivors experience healing as a result of the criminal punishment system, even in the rare cases when the person who caused them harm is found responsible for their behavior (Decker et al., 2019). Because the system relies on external interpretation of an experience of harm or violence, rather than the person who caused harm taking responsibility for it, many survivors do not feel heard, validated, or healed because the person who caused the violence still has not acknowledged or admitted that they caused harm. Punishment is passive; accountability is active (Sered, 2019).

In the next section, I illustrate the ways that deep-rooted racism and carcerality in criminal legal systems also influence campus policies and practices related to addressing sexual misconduct. In particular, I focus on federal policies guiding campus response, including campus adjudication processes and survivor support services.

CAMPUS SEXUAL VIOLENCE POLICY IN A US CONTEXT

Three federal laws inform the ways colleges and universities in the US respond to sexual violence: Title IX, the Clery Act, and the Campus SaVE Act (Duncan, 2014; Dunn, 2014). Policymakers have interpreted and reinterpreted Title IX many times in an attempt to provide guidance for campus sexual misconduct adjudication processes, and the Clery Act has been revised numerous times through the reauthorization of the Violence Against Women Act (VAWA; Dunn, 2014). The Campus SaVE Act, passed as part of the 2013 reauthorization of VAWA, attempted to codify some aspects of the guidance related to the interpretation of Title IX as a law addressing sexual misconduct (Duncan, 2014). A review of each of these laws is beyond the scope of this chapter; however, since Title IX is used as the primary law guiding the ways campuses address sexual misconduct through adjudication, I provide a brief history of Title IX and its many interpretations here.

In the US, the federal government relies on Title IX as the primary mechanism for addressing sexual violence among college students. Passed in 1972, the purpose of Title IX was to ensure gender equity in education in the US. Title IX applies to any educational system that receives federal funding, including K-12 schools and colleges and universities (Boschert, 2022; Tani, 2017). One of the most noted impacts of Title IX on schools and colleges is that it increased the number of opportunities for girls and women to participate in sports in schools and colleges (Boschert, 2022; Silbaugh, 2015); however, Title IX has also influenced a number of other school and campus practices, including the ways that educators deal with peer-to-peer and teacher-to-student sexual harassment (Collins, 2016; Silbaugh, 2015; Tani, 2017).

Title VII of the Civil Rights Act of 1964 includes prohibition of sex discrimination, yet when the Act was passed, most people did not think of sexual harassment or sexual assault as a form of sex discrimination (Silbaugh, 2015; Tani, 2017). Sex discrimination primarily focused on equal opportunity for women in the workplace and did not include attention to sexual harassment. Although sexual harassment came to be interpreted as sex discrimination under Title VII in the 1980s (Tani, 2017), it still only applied to the workplace, not to educational settings; therefore Title IX became an important avenue for addressing sexual harassment in educational settings.

Two specific cases in the 1990s significantly influenced the interpretation of Title IX related to sexual harassment in educational settings: *Gesber vs. Lago Vista Independent School District* and *Davis vs. Monroe County Board of Education* (Tani, 2017). The first case, *Gesber*, involved teacher-to-student sexual harassment and resulted in the Court holding that "monetary damages under Title IX were only available if an official who had authority to address the alleged harassment had 'actual knowledge' of it and, in addition, demonstrated 'deliberate indifference' in responding" (Tani, 2017, p. 1861). The *Davis* case involved peer-to-peer sexual harassment, and the court held the same – administrators needed to have knowledge that sexual harassment was happening and deliberately ignore it to be found responsible under the law (Tani, 2017). Although both cases involved situations in K-12 settings, the findings hold for colleges and universities as well: in order to have equal access to educational opportunities, girls and women have a right to environments free of sexual harassment. It is important to note that Title IX has historically been interpreted as a law that protects girls and women from discrimination and harassment, yet men and gender nonconforming people also experience sexual violence. Specifically, transgender and gender nonconforming people experience extremely high rates of sexual violence (Cantor et al., 2019), so relying on a law that centers women and girls may result in less than effective strategies for supporting other people who experience sexual violence.

Although *Gesber* and *Davis* successfully created an avenue for students to use Title IX as a law to hold institutions accountable for effectively responding to sexual assault, they did little to support school and college administrators in effectively preventing sexual harassment and assault because the "actual knowledge" standard resulted in incentivizing administrators to "bury their heads in the sand" (Tani, 2017, p. 1861) so that they would not know about the harassment. Without actual knowledge of harassment, they had no legal responsibility to address it and therefore no liability. Most school and college administrators would likely prefer to prevent sexual harassment from happening in the first place, yet the structure and interpretation of the law related to sexual harassment and assault results in them having little opportunity to do so. For a long period of time, most legal counsel advised school and college administrators to avoid knowledge of harassment so that they did not have a risk of liability under the law.

The advocacy work of student activists and others led the Office of Civil Rights (OCR) to issue additional guidance for schools and universities in relationship to sexual harassment and assault in schools and colleges in 2001 (and again in subsequent years, which I will address later). Although the OCR could not be involved in hearing specific sexual assault cases or determining the responsibility of a person who caused harm, they could hold institutions accountable for having effective and consistent practices for hearing sexual assault cases. The OCR recommended that the US government withhold federal funding or fine colleges and universities for failing to appropriately address sexual violence (Tani, 2017). The OCR indicated that the Supreme Court's rulings in *Gesber* and *Davis* held for private right-to-action but not to the agency's enforcement of Title IX. For example, even if an individual student did not sue a school or college, the OCR could investigate a school or college's response or lack of response to sexual harassment and assault and fine the school for failing to effectively address the problem (Tani, 2017). Further, the OCR's guidance provided insight for schools and colleges about how they could know about sexual harassment or assault. Essentially, the OCR's guidance indicated that schools and colleges had a responsibility to address sexual harassment and assault on their campuses no matter how they learned of it – through formal reports from students or parents or more informal mechanisms including informal reports to teachers, faculty, and staff (Tani, 2017). Additionally, the OCR's guidance required that campuses consider a clear and convincing evidence standard for hearing sexual assault cases and required campuses discontinue the use of nondisclosure statements for victims of assault (Tani, 2017).

The first OCR guidance in 2001 got little attention because the OCR did not actively enforce the policy. However, after another bout of student activism, the Department of Education issued a second set of guidelines in 2011, commonly referred to as the *Dear Colleague Letter (DCL)*. The 2011 version of the guidance set out more specific guidelines for campuses to address sexual violence, including attention to the role of a Title IX Coordinator, expectations for adjudication processes, and requirements for educating campus community members about sexual violence (Tani, 2017). The *DCL* received significant attention from college and university leadership and created sweeping changes to many campuses' adjudication processes.

Campus legal counsel sought to interpret the 2011 *DCL* and quickly implement the recommendations, including identifying a Title IX Coordinator and implementing "prevention" programming on campuses (Tani, 2017). The haste to comply with the new guidance resulted in significant confusion for many campuses, including confusion about who should serve in the role of a Title IX Coordinator, whether survivors could still access confidential services on campus, and whether campus judicial offices and boards should continue hearing sexual assault cases. Although the *DCL* certainly contributed to a shift in the culture related to addressing sexual assault by centering victims in campus adjudication processes, it also caused a significant amount of confusion for students and administrators alike (Anderson, 2016). Many campuses have centralized the adjudication process to a Title IX Coordinator as recommended in the guidance, which led to greater confusion for students because it is different from where and how students report other kinds of student conduct code violations.

In 2014, the Department of Education issued a Q&A, which attempted to provide more clarity related to sexual misconduct response, especially with regard to responsible employees' duty to report (Bauer-Wolf, 2024). In 2017, newly appointed Secretary of Education Betsy DeVos rescinded the 2011 guidelines and issued interim guidelines focusing largely on loosening the standard of evidence campus adjudication processes were required to use and allowing mediation as a response. In 2020, the Department of Education issued new guidelines as federal rule, requiring live hearings for Title IX cases and introducing additional protections for students accused of causing harm (Bauer-Wolf, 2024; Marine & Hurtado, 2021). In 2024, after several delays, the Department of Education issued a new set of guidelines that addressed both the sexual misconduct processes and protections for transgender students.

The administrative guidelines, or rules, are administrative in nature, meaning that they can be changed at any time by new leadership in the administration of the federal government (Tani, 2017). Interpreting Title IX has become a partisan issue, with the rules changing with each new presidential administration, oscillating between more protections for survivors and more protections for respondents (Marine & Hurtado, 2021). Further, the rules also include provisions for the protection of transgender students in schools and universities, which have made the rules even more partisan, with governors in many states refusing to comply with the new Title IX guidelines as they relate to allowing transgender students to access bathrooms and sports teams that align with their gender (Knott, 2024). Even as someone who works to stay up-to-date with federal policies impacting sexual misconduct, I find the constantly changing of rules, policies, and procedures head-spinning. Just as university administrators begin to get a handle on how to implement the guidelines, they change again, resulting in confusion for all involved. If university administrators and lawyers cannot keep up with the constantly changing guidelines, how could we expect students, who these guidelines are supposed to protect, to be effectively protected?

The use of Title IX as a law to address sexual misconduct has unintentionally contributed to a culture of compliance over a culture of prevention on college campuses. The potential of "severe financial liability" for failing to address sexual misconduct leads university administrators to interpret Title IX "through a discourse of risk management" (Collins, 2016, p. 375), which shifts the focus from collective responsibility for ending violence to an individual responsibility (another byproduct of white supremacy and carcerality).

Although most university administrators certainly want to end violence, the construction and interpretation of laws used to address sexual misconduct facilitates a focus on reducing financial liability, often at the expense of violence prevention (Collins, 2016; Silbaugh, 2015; Tani, 2017), which I explore in more detail in Chapter 5. In the next section, I explore the current interpretation of Title IX's impact on campus adjudication processes and providing support for survivors.

Campus Adjudication Processes

Although campus adjudication systems are independent from the criminal punishment system, Title IX guidance results in adjudication processes being set up in a similar manner as criminal punishment systems (Collins, 2016). Even though Title IX is a civil law, "many universities have embraced the notion that the primary way to demonstrate that they take sexual assault seriously is to punish individuals accused of such offenses harshly and swiftly" (Collins, 2016, p. 367). Carceral feminism, a movement focused on the increased criminalization of sexual violence, has led to the individualization of response to sexual misconduct on college campuses. Largely hailed as a "feminist victory," the increased criminalization of sexualized crimes, including domestic violence, sexual assault, and stalking, carceral feminism focuses on punishment as a primary deterrent for preventing future sexual violence (Goodmark, 2021; Kim, 2018). Given high rates of sexual violence, even with increased criminalization, no evidence exists to support the assumption that increased punishment results in decreased rates of sexual violence (Cantor et al., 2019; Muehlenhard et al., 2017).

Much like carceral criminal punishment systems, adjudication processes favor people with dominant identities – people used to working within systems for fair and impartial accountability. Members of minoritized communities are just as skeptical of campus authority and adjudication processes as they are of community ones because they are so similar in nature (Wallace et al., 2024). Further, as guidance related to Title IX adjudication processes has evolved over time, the recommended processes have come to resemble criminal punishment system procedures (Collins, 2016). Historically, student conduct offices, staffed by student affairs professionals, addressed sexual misconduct as a part of the student code of conduct. Similar to other student conduct issues, student conduct officers addressed sexual misconduct through a lens of accountability *and* student development (Anderson, 2016).

As guidance related to Title IX began to focus more on the sexual misconduct adjudication processes, those processes became more legalistic in nature, largely mimicking the criminal punishment system (Collins, 2016). Sexual misconduct processes moved away from accountability *and* student development to legalistic processes focused on reducing institutional liability for failing to effectively address sexual misconduct (Anderson, 2016; Cruz, 2021). The processes moved away from being managed by student affairs professionals with specific training in student development to attorneys, with a focus on institutional risk management (Anderson, 2016). Even Title IX professionals feel limited in their ability to be effective in their work, noting that no one – respondents nor complainants – benefit from the legalistic, administrative process that mimics a carceral process (Cruz, 2021). Further, the current Title IX processes have not led to a reduction of sexual violence among college students (Cantor et al., 2019; Muehlenhard et al., 2017).

Although one of the purposes of engaging campus adjudication processes whether or not a complainant-survivor chooses to report to the criminal punishment system is to provide some quicker resolution to the issue for both the complainant and respondent, that often does not happen (Cantalupo, 2012). The cumbersome rules for adjudicating a sexual misconduct case, which mimic the criminal punishment system, draw out the process, providing little respite for the complainant-survivor. Campus adjudication process sometimes drag on for months at a time. Further, because campuses are their own communities with their own standards, advocates of campus processes also argue that they can have higher standards for behavior than the general community (Cantalupo, 2012). For example, although the criminal punishment system requires a "beyond a reasonable doubt" standard because the consequences of being found responsible for a felony may include jail time, the standard for a campus system may be more likely than not (depending on which iteration of the Title IX guidance is in place) because the consequences for being held responsible for a violation of the code of conduct may be suspension or expulsion but that does not infringe upon a person's freedom. Because it is a privilege, rather than a right, to access colleges and university campuses who all have their own sets of admissions standards, universities may have higher standards for behavior.

Survivor Support

Policy, and the interpretation of it, play a significant role in the ways campus structures support (or not) survivors of sexual violence. In addition to the rules and requirements related to campus adjudication processes, federal policy also mandates victim-survivor support and responsible employee reporting, two practices often in conflict with each other (Dunn, 2014).

Federal guidance related to Title IX, The Clery Act, and the Campus SaVE Act all require campuses to provide support for victim-survivors of sexual violence (Duncan, 2014; Dunn, 2014). Although the interpretation of what support might look like varies from campus to campus, many campuses either have victim-survivor advocates on campus or contract with off-campus victim-survivor organizations to provide advocacy for survivors. In most states, at least some of these advocacy services remain confidential services for survivors (Marine & Hurtado, 2021), meaning that if survivors choose to engage victim-survivor advocacy, they do not also have to report their experience to campus Title IX officials.

However, as university administrators and legal counsel continue to interpret sexual misconduct policy through a risk management lens, confidential spaces for survivors are at risk (Holland et al., 2018). Even when victim-survivor advocacy centers have confidentiality privilege, many university legal counsel require that these offices report the numbers of survivors they see and require that they report certain instances of sexual violence to campus authorities.

Federal guidance related to Title IX has also led to increased attention on responsible employee reporting. Again, as interpreted through a risk management lens, Title IX requires institutional leaders to take action if they know or should have known about incidents of sexual violence directed at students (Holland et al., 2018). Because university employees represent the university when acting in the official capacity of their jobs, a risk management perspective interprets Title IX to imply that employees have a duty to report incidents of violence to university administration – in this case, a Title IX office. While certainly on this surface this makes sense to ensure that students receive the support they need to navigate the aftermath of an incident of violence and to attempt to prevent future violence by intervening with the person who caused harm, the reality is much more complicated than that. Requiring employees to report any incident of violence shared with them to university administration is not a trauma-informed practice (Holland et al., 2021; Larson, 2023). Trauma-informed practices necessitate that the person who experienced harm is in control of their experience after the harm occurs, and someone else reporting their experience without their consent removes that control. Students describe mandatory reporting by responsible employees as a form of institutional betrayal (Gartner et al., 2024). When students believe that they are sharing a personal experience with a trusted mentor for support and validation, that trust is revoked when the employee must report the incident to the Title IX office (Gartner et al., 2024; Larson, 2023). Although most Title IX offices do not act without the consent or involvement of a person who has experienced harm, the loss of control of even making this report has significant negative impacts on the healing of the person who experienced harm.

Not only is the practice of mandated reporting not trauma-informed, it also rarely results in the intended outcome (Holland et al., 2018). Because campus adjudication processes are so cumbersome and legalistic, most survivors do not choose to participate in an adjudication process, making it impossible to intervene with the person who caused harm. Failing to intervene with the person who caused harm does not prevent future violence from occurring. Further, mandatory reporting creates a chilling effect on the relationship between faculty and students and staff and students, resulting in students not getting the support that they need from trusted mentors (Holland et al., 2021; Larson, 2023). If students understand that faculty and staff have a duty to report any incident of violence to campus administrators whom the students do not know, they will be less likely to share their experience and get the help they need. Additionally, many faculty and staff do not want to be put in the position of reporting, so they do not engage in conversations with students that may lead to any disclosures of violence (Holland et al., 2021), resulting in further silence and shame around sexual violence.

Carceral practices have also had a chilling effect on spaces that have historically provided respite and community for survivors of violence. For example, many women's centers on college campuses in the US established in the 1970s and 1980s included an explicit focus on addressing sexual violence (Cottledge et al., 2015). Staff in these centers worked to support survivors, advocate for survivors at the institutional level, and raise awareness about interpersonal violence across the institution and beyond. Additionally, many staff in these offices worked to navigate a political minefield that could potentially cause more harm to survivors they strove to support. Knowing that formal campus adjudication systems and criminal punishment systems were less than effective at addressing issues of sexual violence, advocates in women's centers worked to educate those within these formal systems at the same time they worked to protect survivors from institutional betrayal or further harm by systems. Now, staff in women's or gender centers (if they still exist) are considered "responsible employees," requiring them to report disclosures of sexual violence to a Title IX office. Mandatory reporting has led to previously safe spaces, like women's centers, not being safe for survivors of sexual violence because if they report their experience with sexual violence to a staff person there, the staff person must report it to the institution and the survivor loses the choice they had as to whether or not they wanted to engage in a formal reporting process (Engle, 2015; Holland et al., 2018).

CONCLUSION

Carcerality – using police, prisons, and policy – to control people has roots in racism and classism. Although campus sexual misconduct adjudication processes are separate from criminal punishment systems, campus processes also subscribe to carceral approaches for addressing violence. Carceral approaches neither eradicate violence nor allow students to heal from their traumatic experiences. In fact, most sexual misconduct processes cause further trauma for victim-survivors and not provide opportunities for people who caused harm to engage in their own healing to prevent future violence. Even in the rare cases a person is found responsible for causing harm to another person, few opportunities for accountability exist. A person who causes harm may be punished or removed from the institution, but they do not learn from nor take responsibility for repairing the harm they caused. A culture of compliance results in university administrators engaging in practice to avoid liability or "getting in trouble" from the federal government rather than engaging in practices that are healing for students and address the culture that allows violence to thrive. In the next chapter, I turn to examining strategies for preventing sexual violence among college students.

5

PREVENTION OF SEXUAL VIOLENCE AMONG COLLEGE STUDENTS

ABSTRACT

In this chapter, I define primary prevention as stopping violence before it happens. First, I describe the differences between learning and training to set a context for this chapter. I then examine the evolution of sexual violence education programs on college campuses, dividing programs into five major categories. Finally, I conclude the chapter describing the research about people who engage in harmful behavior advocate for more prevention strategies focused directly on people who may or have caused harm.

Keywords: Sexual violence; primary prevention; educational programs; training and mandatory reporting; risk factors for harmful sexual behavior

Although many people who work on college and university campuses classify most activities related to addressing campus sexual violence as a form of prevention, actual prevention work focuses on stopping sexual violence before it happens (American College Health Association [ACHA], 2008) rather than responding to it after it happens. Preventing violence requires educators and administrators to focus on interrupting harm in addition to risk reduction. Many educational programs focus explicitly, and almost exclusively, on risk reduction strategies or teaching people who may be targeted for violence how to avoid violence (Kettrey et al., 2023). While important, risk reduction strategies focus on sexual violence as an individual issue and place responsibility for stopping violence on people targeted for violence. Risk reduction does not end violence – it simply reorganizes it. When we do not intervene with a person who has or may cause harm, we do not end violence – we just stop one specific instance of violence from happening. Primary prevention relies on the philosophy that "sexual violence is not inevitable, and can be prevented by making changes to societal norms surrounding sexuality, violence, gender, and oppression" (ACHA, 2008, p. 7). Focusing on interrupting harm by teaching people what harmful behavior is so that they do not perpetuate it may be a more effective way to end violence.

As outlined in Chapter 4, most legislation and policy related to sexual violence do not allow administrators and educators to focus on primary prevention of sexual violence; instead, policy requires them to develop more effective procedures for responding to sexual violence after it occurs, which often takes away from resources to engage in innovative prevention strategies (Collins, 2016; Linder, Karunaratne, & Grimes, 2024; Silbaugh, 2015). Although some would argue that effective response to sexual violence will result in a reduction of sexual violence because people who cause harm will be less likely to engage in sexual violence if they believe they will be held accountable for their actions, statistics do not support this notion. Although rates of incarceration for sexual violence have increased (Travis et al., 2014), rates of sexual victimization have not decreased (Cantor et al., 2019; Muehlenhard et al., 2017). Effective response to sexual violence is an important piece of the puzzle to eradicate sexual violence, yet it should not supersede prevention initiatives focused on intervening with people at risk for engaging in harmful sexual behavior.

In this chapter, I focus on two primary prevention strategies: educating students about violence and interrupting harm by intervening with those who have or may cause harm. First, I describe the differences between education and training to set a context for this chapter. I then examine the evolution of sexual violence education programs on college campuses, including the research and evaluation practices commonly used to examine the effectiveness of the programs. I use a power-conscious lens to highlight ways well-intended educational programs may unintentionally harm some students, including people targeted for sexual violence. Finally, I conclude the chapter describing the research about people who engage in harmful behavior to advocate for more prevention strategies to focus directly on people who may or have caused harm.

EDUCATION AND "MANDATORY TRAINING"

Taking note of the over-emphasis on response, some policies, including the Campus SAVE Act, require campuses to provide education related to sexual violence for all students (Collins, 2016; Duncan, 2014). The educational requirements of the Campus SAVE Act are "largely reactive: the programs assume that sexual assault will be attempted or will occur and put the onus on potential victims and bystanders to prevent it" (Collins, 2016, p. 383). Specifically, the Campus SAVE Act requires

> *[...]schools to implement programs that educate students about 'risk reduction to recognize warning signs of abusive behavior and how to avoid potential attacks' and 'safe and positive options for bystander intervention that may be carried out by an individual to prevent harm or intervene when there is a risk of [...] sexual assault.'*
>
> (Collins, 2016, p. 383)

The requirements codified by the Campus SAVE Act illustrate the challenges associated with prevention education on college campuses – the assumption that violence can and will occur, with little understanding of how to actually prevent violence. Even at institutions of higher education, where one of our primary missions is education, most of us do not believe we can effectively intervene with and re-educate people who have or may engage in harmful sexual behavior.

Most campus administrators have translated the mandate of required education for all students to a "mandatory training" requirement. In fact, many student activists and researchers also advocate for "mandatory training" for all incoming students (Worthen & Wallace, 2021, p. 2642). The term *mandatory training* is another ubiquitous term, used frequently among educators, administrators, and activists, yet rarely do we examine the effectiveness of *mandatory* training. As most educators know, training and learning are two dramatically different things (Kulbaga & Spencer, 2019). Training focuses on teaching people something very specific. I might need training to use a new learning management system or a new system for tracking vacation hours of my employees

– things that are very specific and a quick video can show me which buttons to click. I do not need to understand the inner workings of the technology, nor the philosophy behind it, to approve my staff members' time off.

Learning, on the other hand, focuses on creating opportunities for people to make sense of a new idea or concept and how to apply it in their specific contexts (Mezirow, 1997). A learning environment focuses on teaching people what questions to ask and what makes sense in different contexts, rather than specifically what to do or think. Providing opportunities for learning (rather than training) about the dynamics of sexual violence may be far more effective at shifting the culture around violence (Kulbaga & Spencer, 2019). When educators provide students with the space to consider a continuum of harm, of how different people may experience similar behaviors in different ways, they gain empathy and understanding. They may recognize that they need to check in with their partner's comfort before proceeding with sexual activity, rather than assuming. *Training* related to sexual violence focuses on explaining policies about sexual misconduct to students, or clearcut definitions of consent, but does not leave room for students to wrestle with their own understandings of harm and boundaries. When trainings focus on legal and policy definitions, we miss the opportunity to help students understand and think through the nuance of interacting with their peers and to consider harmful behaviors that do not meet the legal or policy definition of sexual misconduct or sexual assault.

Similarly, the mandatory aspect of the training warrants increased attention. I often ask rooms full of administrators when they learned something from a "mandatory training." I get lots of smirks. When we consider our own experiences, most of us realize that attempting to require someone to learn something often backfires. Most of us resist being told what or how to think and get defensive about required training. Researchers have also documented the impact of required training about sexual violence among students. Trainings may perpetuate a boomerang effect, making students more likely to engage in harmful behavior (Malamuth et al., 2018). Alternatively, some students may experience defensiveness and resist the message altogether (Nicolla & Lazard, 2023). Unfortunately, this research has been conducted with men only, so we know less about the resistance to mandatory education for people of other genders.

Additionally, because we all start from different places and have different experiences with different topics, generic trainings are often less than helpful and feel condescending to people receiving the training (Worthen & Wallace, 2021; Worthen & Wallace, 2017). People do not engage in harmful sexual behavior because they do not know that there is a policy prohibiting it; they engage in harmful sexual behavior either because they do not understand that what they're doing constitutes harm or because they do not care if they are harming another person. Neither of these is something we can address by letting someone know about a policy. Further, when I ask what assessment we have done to determine what people are learning or taking from mandatory trainings, I often receive the response, "it's a best practice."

As with other federal laws, the required education component of federal laws sets administrators up to focus on complying with the law through a "best practice," rather than thinking through what effective education might look like on their specific campuses. Because education about sexual violence is one of many mandates university administrators manage, finding a straightforward way to comply with it makes sense. As with most legal requirements, the educational component then becomes an issue of compliance, rather than education. A few big companies make millions of dollars off selling prepackaged, online educational modules to universities (Kulbaga & Spencer, 2019; Smith, 2015), fulfilling the statutory requirement. However, minimal assessment about the effectiveness of these programs exist.

Campus administrators, educators, and researchers know little about the effectiveness of most educational programs and workshops. Most educational programs have not been effectively evaluated to determine their impact on the prevalence of sexual violence on college campuses (Kettry et al., 2023; Newlands & O'Donohue, 2016; Wright et al., 2020). Evaluation of programs consistently focus on students' satisfaction with the program or measure changes in their attitudes and beliefs about sexual violence, but do not actually measure changes in the prevalence of sexual violence (Anderson & Whiston, 2005; Kettry et al., 2023; Newlands & O'Donohue, 2016; Vladutiu et al., 2010). Further, most programs are evaluated in a one-time capacity, resulting in little information about the long-term efficacy of the programs (Kettry et al., 2023; Newlands & O'Donohue, 2016).

In lieu of effective evaluation of educational programs, educators and administrators frequently focus on "best" or "promising" practices to develop their educational strategies. Some organizations note the challenges of evaluating educational programs, and highlight rationale for "promising directions," which includes an "expected effect of the program because it is based on sound theory and previous research" (Culture of Respect, n.d., para 3). Unfortunately, given the history of failing to account for power and identity in research, this means that many of the practices considered "promising" are likely based on dominant ideas related to sexual violence, including the over-reliance on teaching people targeted for sexual violence how not to get assaulted, rather than teaching people who may cause sexual harm not to harm (Kettry et al., 2023). Further, most "promising" or "best" practices focus on dominant group members and fail to consider the experiences of people with minoritized identities, including people of color, people with disabilities, and queer and transgender people (Chugani et al., 2021; Wooten, 2017; Worthen & Wallace, 2017, 2021; Zounlome et al., 2019). Finally, best practices usually address a symptom of a problem, rather than shifting the underlying frameworks that cause the problem in the first place (Nicolazzo, 2016).

HISTORY AND EVOLUTION OF CAMPUS SEXUAL VIOLENCE EDUCATION

Activists and educators have been working to educate students about campus sexual violence for decades although most documented evaluation of these programs emerged in the 1980s and 1990s (Brecklin & Forde, 2001). Consistent with the histories of most minoritized groups, educational programs related to sexual violence on college campuses originally emerged from consciousness-raising groups of the 1970s (Bohmer & Parrot, 1993). Because campus administrators were not yet addressing sexual violence on campus, feminist activists and educators frequently took the lead in educating women about the risks of sexual violence, including strategies for reducing their risk. Although feminists knew it was not the responsibility of potential victims to end sexual violence, they also knew that the opportunities to intervene with people at risk for engaging in harmful sexual behaviors were limited because of the immense power that dominant groups hold and the lack of understanding of the dynamics of sexual violence as a crime of power and dominance (Brownmiller, 1993; Warshaw, 1994). As more people began to understand the significance of sexual violence on college campuses, educational programs evolved and have become integrated into campus policies and practices.

One of the greatest challenges in educating students, faculty, and staff about sexual violence are the varied definitions and understandings of sexual violence. Researchers use a variety of terms and definitions to understand students' experiences with sexual violence, resulting in lack of clarity around the prevalence of physical sexual violence and strategies for educating students about assault, especially for students with minoritized identities (deHeer & Jones, 2017; Wood et al., 2017). For example, researchers use the terms *unwanted sexual touching*, *sexual coercion*, *incapacitated rape*, *forcible rape*, and *sexual assault* to examine prevalence of sexual violence. As one might imagine, attempting to address each of these types of violence in educational programming for college students presents a significant challenge. Even if educators use language accessible to students, helping students to understand the wide variety of experiences with sexual violence requires time to explore complex and nuanced concepts (Linder, Richards, et al., 2024). Time is typically not available to sexual violence educators who are expected to complete their work in one-time presentations at orientation or through online modules that combine education about high-risk alcohol use and sexual violence. In addition to the differences between technical terms related to sexual violence, educators must also navigate ways to address the differences between harmful and illegal behaviors, consistently reminding students that something doesn't have to be illegal to be harmful.

Educational programs related to sexual violence have ranged from teaching people targeted for sexual violence (mostly women) self-defense and other strategies for reducing their risk of sexual violence to interrupting common myths that people have about sexual violence to teaching people bystander intervention skills (heavily focused on men) in hopes that people will intervene when they see potentially dangerous situations (Kettrey et al., 2023; Newlands & O'Donohue, 2016; Wright et al., 2020). Throughout all these strategies, educators weave a strand of teaching students about the risks of heavy drinking, leading to confusing messages about the role of alcohol in sexual violence. Unfortunately, very few programs directly intervene with people engaged in harmful behavior or at risk for engaging in harmful behavior to address sexual violence. Most programs focused on engaging men focus on them as allies to address sexual violence, rather than as targets for experiencing violence or people who may cause harm (Wright et al., 2020). Failing to directly engage people who have or may engage in harmful sexual behavior results in less-than-effective strategies for preventing sexual violence on college campuses.

Further, many educators facilitate sexual violence education workshops from an identity-neutral perspective, meaning that they fail to consider the role of power, privilege, and identity in sexual violence educational programming (Chugani et al., 2021; Wooten, 2017; Worthen & Wallace, 2017, 2021; Zounlome et al., 2019). Many workshops on sexual violence center cisgender, heterosexual, nondisabled white women as the primary victims of sexual violence, rendering other potential victims invisible (Wooten, 2017; Worthen & Wallace, 2017; Zounlome et al., 2019). The failure of educators and administrators to consider power and dominance as the underlying cause of sexual violence results in ineffective educational programs to eradicate sexual violence on college campuses.

A review of the literature indicates that most sexual violence educational programs fall into five major categories: (1) single-gender programs directed at women as potential targets, (2) single-gender programs directed at men as potential allies and bystanders, (3) mixed-gender programs focused on defining sexual violence and dispelling rape myths, (4) bystander intervention programs directed at men or mixed-gender groups, and (5) programs designed to reduce the risk of sexual violence by teaching students about the role of alcohol in sexual violence. In the following sections, I provide an overview and power conscious-critique of educational programs in each of these categories, illuminating considerations for administrators and educators when implementing educational programs related to sexual violence.

Single-Gender Programs Directed at Women as Potential Victims

Rooted in the tension somewhere between feminist consciousness-raising and chivalrous attempts to protect women, many prevention programs take the form of risk reduction programs directed toward women as potential victims. These programs may consist of self-defense workshops aimed at teaching women how to physically defend themselves or develop strategies for verbally resisting assault (Hollander, 2014) and setting boundaries. Some risk-reduction programs directed at women as potential victims also include attention to high-risk drinking (Clinton-Sherrod et al., 2011). Although alcohol is correlated with sexual violence, it is not the cause of sexual violence. In fact, researchers indicate that alcohol only exacerbates the sociocultural factors surrounding sexual violence on college campuses, rather than creating the sociocultural factors (Gray et al., 2017). In other words, even if college students reduce their rates of high-risk drinking, sexual violence would not end. Factors associated with power, entitlement, and gender-role ideology contribute to a culture of sexual violence more than alcohol (Wright et al., 2020).

Finally, a few programs have focused on teaching women signs of people at risk of causing harm, attempting to provide them tools to identify potentially risky situations.

Although educational programs focused on people as targets of violence are an important component of a comprehensive educational program, if implemented haphazardly or without attention to power, they may contribute to a culture of victim-blaming or perpetuating the notion that women – or any potential victims – are responsible for ending sexual violence. They may also send the message that people who cause harm only target women as potential victims, rather than acknowledging the ways that men and nonbinary people also experience sexual violence. Further, if organized and implemented without appropriate nuance, these programs may contribute to perpetuating myths about sexual violence. For example, many self-defense workshops focus on stranger danger, teaching women to protect themselves from a potential sudden attack. Most cases of sexual violence among college students are perpetrated by someone known to the victim (Cantor et al., 2019), and often in a dating or social situation in which it would be unlikely that a potential victim would use physical self-defense tactics. Focusing heavily on self-defense perpetuates misinformation about the dynamics of sexual violence, potentially contributing to a culture in which potential victims are unaware of accurate signs of potential harmful sexual behavior.

Given that people who engage in sexual violence target women and nonbinary people at alarmingly high rates (Cantor et al., 2019), it is important to focus on women and nonbinary people as potential targets for sexual violence. However, exclusively focusing on women as potential victims also contributes to a culture in which men and nonbinary people are not considered people who experience harm, resulting in them not being believed when they report experiences of sexual violence, or even seeing themselves as potential targets.

Programs focused on identifying the strategies that people who cause harm use to target victims may be the most promising of programs focused on potential targets for sexual violence, yet they must be implemented through a power-conscious lens that recognizes a variety of people as potential targets of sexual violence. Unfortunately, most programs focused on potential victims and risk reduction focus on high-risk alcohol use and self-defense and are directed almost exclusively toward women (Kettrey et al., 2023).

Single-Gender Programs Directed at Men as Potential Allies and Bystanders

In the 1990s, as attention to campus sexual violence grew and as feminists made clear the responsibility for ending sexual violence lies with people who cause harm (Warshaw, 1994), not targets of harm, educators began to implement single-sex programming directed at men. Programs like One in Four, The Men's Project, and the Men's Program emerged on college campuses (Hong, 2000). The purpose of these programs was to engage men as allies in addressing campus sexual violence. The philosophy underlying these programs is that most men are "good" men, meaning that they would not commit sexual violence, but that they frequently interact with peers who do commit sexual violence (Hong, 2000). Based on research that indicates that most people who engage in sexual violence do so more than once (Abbey et al., 2007), the intent of educational programs targeting men was to teach them effective strategies for intervening with their male peers who exhibited signs of hostility toward women and who may engage in sexual violence. More recent scholarship has challenged the notion that people who engage in sexual violence do so more than once, resulting in the need to examine the philosophy underlying many of these programs (Gray et al., 2017).

Educational programs directed at men often focused on teaching them about sexual violence by assuming they were not causing harm and could intervene with people who did cause harm (Wright et al., 2020). Unfortunately, this philosophy resulted in ignoring research that clearly exemplified that there are some patterns of harmful sexual behavior and that some risk factors, do indeed, allow educators and administrators to identify people who may be at higher risk of committing sexual violence. Although it is likely not helpful to approach all men as people who engage in sexual violence, it is also unhelpful to ignore what we do know about people who have or may engage in acts of sexual violence. Few educators and administrators avoid developing programs directed at people who are considered high-risk for experiencing sexual violence, yet those same educators and administrators avoid approaching people who are at high-risk for causing sexual violence. In the second half of this chapter, I explore risk factors for harmful sexual behavior to shed light on possible ways to effectively identify people at risk for causing harm.

Programs that unilaterally focus on men as potential allies to end sexual violence also run the risk of causing further harm by perpetuating enlightened sexism or engaging in behaviors that appear to be egalitarian but are actually harmful to women (Armato, 2013). In fact, bystander intervention programs often perpetuate the notion that women need men to protect them and that men cannot be victims of sexual violence, which are ironically, two beliefs that form the foundation for a rape-supportive culture. Programs focused on men as potential allies may also result in increased rates of sexual violence by providing people who cause harm with a shield to protect them from being identified as a someone who engages in sexual violence. Some men have used their participation in men's programs to get closer to their potential targets to cause harm (Linder & Johnson, 2015).

Mixed-Gender Programs Focused on General Sexual Violence Education

Another strategy that educators have used since the 1990s includes general education programs about sexual violence that target all students. The purpose of these programs is to teach students definitions and understandings of sexual violence, interrupt myths about sexual violence, and develop empathy for survivors of sexual violence (Brecklin & Forde, 2001; Kettrey et al., 2023; Newlands & O'Donohue, 2016). Feminists and sociologists in the 1970s argued that people's acceptance of myths related to sexual violence led to a culture in which many people blamed victims for being assaulted and minimized and ignored the behaviors of those who engaged in sexual violence, resulting in a hostile climate for survivors of sexual violence. This hostile climate also resulted in survivors not disclosing their experiences of violence, resulting in fewer opportunities for healing (Burt, 1980; Malamuth, 1989; Murnen et al., 2002).

Research on general education programs indicates that participants generally experience a decline in rape myth acceptance immediately after the program, but the results of the long-term effects of these programs are mixed (Anderson & Whiston, 2005; Kettrey et al., 2023; Newlands & O'Donohue, 2016). Further, little is known about the actual behavior change of people engaged in sexual violence education workshops. It is difficult to measure decreased rates of sexual violence as an outcome of educational workshops. Researchers typically measure attitudes and beliefs about rape and sexual violence, which some researchers have connected to propensity to rape, although the connection is mixed (Anderson & Whiston, 2005; Brecklin & Forde, 2001; Newlands & O'Donohue, 2016; Vladutiu et al., 2010). However, one thing is clear: despite educators' best efforts at reaching college students in a variety of educational workshops, rates of sexual victimization on college campuses have not changed in 60 years (Muehlenhard et al., 2017).

Given that most education programs are designed from a generic, one-size-fits-all perspective, it is not surprising that they fail to reach most students. Students frequently believe the information does not apply to them or that no one they know is a victim or person who would cause harm so they do not make meaning of the information in ways that stick (Worthen & Wallace, 2017). Further, given that people who engage in harmful sexual behavior target minoritized populations at higher rates than their dominant group peers (Cantor et al., 2019), educational programs must illustrate the complexities of sexual violence as a tool of power and domination exerted over more than just heterosexual cisgender white middle-class women (Karunaratne & Harris, 2022; Wooten, 2017; Worthen & Wallace, 2017). Dynamics of sexual violence look different for different populations, and those dynamics should be included throughout educational programs. Although some educators indicate that an "easy way to do this" (Culture of Respect, 2017, p. 52) is to use gender-neutral pronouns and visible people of color in their educational materials, this is only the first step in addressing the complexity of sexual violence. Because the dynamics of oppression impact people differently based on their social identities, simply replacing white students with students of color in videos, marketing materials, and skits, or using gender-neutral pronouns, will not address these complex dynamics. For example, sexual violence between two women looks very different than sexual violence between a man and a woman – failing to address these dynamics in educational programs does a disservice to all involved. Unfortunately, there is no "easy" way to address sexual violence and its complex, nuanced dynamics. To educate students effectively about sexual violence, educators and administrators must make a commitment to move beyond one-time required educational programs and integrate accurate information about the dynamics of power, privilege, oppression, and sexual violence into the curriculum, policies, and practices of the institution. I will explore the specifics of this in more detail in Chapter 6.

Bystander Intervention Programs

Rooted in the philosophy that addressing sexual violence requires a community approach, bystander intervention programs emerged in the early 2000s (Banyard et al., 2004). Bystander intervention moves beyond the individual level approach to addressing sexual violence, requiring members of a community to understand and address behaviors that may lead to sexual violence and to appropriately support survivors who disclose experiences with sexual violence. Combining community readiness models with bystander intervention strategies, researchers and educators believed that bystander intervention programs showed promise for addressing sexual assault on college campuses (Banyard et al., 2004). Specifically, because most campuses pride themselves on being a "community," researchers and educators believed that bystander intervention would fit well on campuses because of the significance of community in bystander intervention strategies. The philosophy is that when people care about members of the community in which they are engaged, they are more likely to intervene in potentially harmful situations (Banyard et al., 2004).

Unfortunately, bystander intervention programs have yet to demonstrate an impact on actual changes in behavior (Katz & Moore, 2013; McMahon, 2015). Similar to previous educational programs, making a direct connection between bystander intervention trainings and reductions of rates of sexual violence is difficult. Researchers measure the effectiveness of bystander intervention trainings by measuring participants' understanding of sexual violence (knowing when to intervene), knowledge of bystander strategies (ways to intervene), bystander efficacy (confidence and willingness to intervene), and sometimes bystander behavior (actual interventions in the previous two months; Banyard et al., 2009; Kettrey & Marx, 2019; McMahon et al., 2011; Moynihan & Banyard, 2008). As with most research on the effectiveness of educational programs and sexual violence intervention programs, participants self-report their willingness to intervene and their actual attempts at intervening. To date, no research indicates consistent, long-term effectiveness of bystander intervention trainings among college students (Katz & Moore, 2013; McMahon, 2015).

Some scholars and researchers have begun to critique the premise on which bystander intervention was founded as it relates to college campuses. To start, because sexual violence is a complex and nuanced problem, it is difficult to teach students in a brief training session the dynamics of sexual violence and when and how to intervene. Given that most sexual violence situations on college campuses involve acquaintances and some consensual sexual activity (Cantor et al., 2019), it is difficult for bystanders to interpret what is consensual activity and what is not consensual; further, sexual violence frequently takes place in private settings when only the two parties are present, making it difficult for a bystander to intervene (Reid & Dundes, 2017).

Similarly, given the power- and identity-neutral ways in which bystander intervention programs are enacted, students likely have a misunderstanding of who engages in harmful sexual violence. In fact, one study clearly documented that white women were less likely to intervene in situations in which the potential target was a Black woman (Katz et al., 2018). Additionally, because strangers, men of color, and "creepy guys" are frequently portrayed as people who engage in sexual violence (Zounlme et al., 2021), most students do not consider their friends or "good (white) college boys" people who may engage in sexual violence and would, therefore, fail to intervene in many typical instances of sexual violence. Further, given the incongruence of typical bystander intervention programs with a heavy emphasis on heterosexual relationships and high rates of sexual violence among minoritized populations many instances of sexual violence are not even being included in bystander programs (McMahon et al., 2020). Simply replacing heterosexual students with queer students in various scenarios likely will not help this challenge as the dynamics related to sexual violence among queer students are different than those among heterosexual students (Bang et al., 2017; Klein et al., 2023; McMahon et al., 2020).

Bystander intervention programs typically focus on removing a potential target or person who may cause harm from a specific situation, which may stop violence from occurring in that one instance, but it does not address the long-term issues related to violence (Chief Elk & Devereaux, 2014). Without appropriate intervention or education, the person who causes harm will go on to continue causing harm in other places.

Finally, some of the most popular bystander intervention programs conflate high-risk alcohol use and sexual violence, leading to confusing messages for students about their role intervening. I attended one campus's bystander intervention training for students and left feeling confused about where the attention to sexual violence was. The training was primarily about intervening when students had too much to drink, which sometimes related to sexual violence and sometimes did not. Many students in the first-year experience course I taught at this institution attended the bystander intervention training course as one of their required out-of-class experiences and through their reflections, noted the same concerns I did about the heavy emphasis on alcohol and minimal education related to sexual violence. Although the premise of bystander intervention programs makes some sense, the enactment of the programs from a power- and identity-neutral lens results in them being less than effective as a strategy for addressing campus sexual violence.

Addressing High-Risk Alcohol Use as a Strategy for Preventing Sexual Violence

Because high-risk alcohol use is heavily correlated with sexual violence, some educators have developed interventions focused on addressing high-risk alcohol use as a strategy for preventing sexual violence. However, research about the relationship between alcohol and sexual violence is confusing at best. Most research indicates that alcohol is "involved" in a high number of sexual assaults on college campuses (Lawyer et al., 2010; Mohler-Kuo et al., 2004). This "involvement" could be that a victim is too intoxicated to consent (Lawyer et al., 2010); a victim's use of alcohol as a coping mechanism for dealing with previous sexual assault (Testa et al., 2010); a victim's inhibitions are lowered, resulting in them making different decisions related to sexual activity than they would if they had not been drinking (Testa et al., 2006); the person causing harm uses alcohol as a weapon to target their victim (Gray et al., 2017); or the alcohol changes the expectancies related to sexual contact of the person causing harm, resulting in them being more sexually aggressive than they are without alcohol (Abbey & Jacques-Tiura, 2011; Gray et al., 2017).

Despite the confusing nature of the scholarship, it is frequently interpreted as "if we teach college women to drink less, we will see a reduction in sexual violence." In fact, this may or may not be true and the subliminal message sent to students about the role of alcohol in sexual violence is problematic and harmful. Teaching college students (specifically college women) that if they do not drink, or drink responsibly, that they will not be targeted by people who engage in sexual violence perpetuates the notion that potential targets have control over whether or not they are assaulted. Further, focusing on alcohol consumption contributes to minimization and self-blame for survivors of sexual violence, which stagnates their healing after an experience of sexual violence (Ameral et al., 2020; Karunaratne, 2023). Certainly, educators have a responsibility to teach students about the risks associated with alcohol use; however, they can do this without conflating alcohol education with sexual violence education. Both are significant and important issues with different root causes and must be handled accordingly.

In addition to placing an undue responsibility on potential targets of sexual violence to prevent themselves from being assaulted, a heavy focus on alcohol takes responsibility away from people who engage in sexual violence. Researchers indicate that when two college students are drinking prior to a sexual assault, students assign higher responsibility to the person targeted for violence than to the person who caused harm (Untied et al., 2012). Students indicate that the person targeted for harm had a responsibility to reduce their risk of sexual violence by drinking less and the person who caused harm was less responsible for their behavior because they did not know what they were doing because they were drunk (Untied et al., 2012). Educators must interrupt this problematic assumption about the role of alcohol in sexual violence. However, in the culture of one-size-fits-all, quick-fix responses to addressing sexual violence on college campuses, the focus on addressing alcohol as a factor in sexual violence frequently results in a strong emphasis on teaching potential targets of violence to be cautious of how much they drink. Although it is certainly wise for all people to be mindful of their level of intoxication for many health and safety reasons, the gendered nature of this message in many sexual violence education programs perpetuates sexism and potential targets' responsibility for ending sexual violence. In the following section, I examine the research about harmful sexual behavior among college students, providing some insight on developing educational programs focused on interrupting harmful sexual behavior, rather than primarily focusing on risk reduction.

THE PATTERNS OF HARMFUL SEXUAL BEHAVIOR

Many educational programs which constitute most prevention programs on college campuses focus on potential targets and bystanders of sexual violence rather than people who may or have caused sexual harm (Kettrey et al., 2023). Given that primary prevention rests on stopping harmful sexual behavior before it starts, it is important for administrators and educators to consider strategies for directly addressing people who have or may engage in harmful sexual behavior. In Chapter 2,

I examined the relationship between oppression, dominance, violence, and trauma to underscore some reasons why people engage in harmful behavior. In this chapter, I summarize the more traditional research focusing on individual level risk and protective factors for harmful sexual behaviors. Considering multiple perspectives about harmful sexual behavior may lead to more effective strategies for intervening with those who have or may cause harm.

Most research on harmful sexual behavior focuses on men who assault women, providing little information on other kinds of sexual violence. Between 12 and 14.2% of college men report engaging in at least one act of sexual violence in the previous year (Gray et al., 2017), with some studies documenting up to 23% of men engaging in coercive sexual behavior (Zinzow & Thompson, 2015). Although I critiqued the method in which research about harmful sexual behavior has been conducted, I also believe it is important to consider this research for insight into potential strategies for intervening with those who have or may cause harm. Researchers have identified some factors associated with harmful sexual behavior, including individual characteristics and socio-cultural environmental factors (Gray et al., 2017). At this point, this research exclusively focuses on men, so I use the term "men who cause harm" rather than "people who cause harm" in this section.

Researchers suggest that the high rates of sexual violence on college campuses are caused by two types of men engaged in sexual violence: repeat behaviors from men who begin causing sexual harm in adolescence and develop patterns over time and one-time opportunistic behaviors from men who are attempting to "conform to masculine expectations" exacerbated by alcohol (Gray et al., 2017, p. 50). Although alcohol is associated with sexual violence in literature about perpetration and victimization risk factors, a more nuanced review of the literature suggests that alcohol likely exacerbates the individual and sociocultural factors already at play on college campuses contributing to high rates of sexual violence. For example, men who already possess the individual traits that make them at risk for engaging in sexual violence are more likely to do so after drinking because the alcohol contributes to a decrease in inhibitions and beliefs that their behavior will result in negative consequences (Abbey & Jacques-Tiura, 2011; Gray et al., 2017; Zinzow & Thompson, 2015).

Individual-level factors associated with harmful sexual behavior include developmental risk factors and pathological personality traits. Specifically, men who experienced physical and/or sexual abuse in childhood, witnessed domestic violence, and have poor parental attachment (learning that expression of their emotions will not result in comfort from their parents) are at higher risk for committing sexual violence (Gray et al., 2017). Additionally, rape myth acceptance, hostility toward women, sexist beliefs, antisocial personality traits, being a victim of physical dating violence, substance use, and frequency of hookups all appear as "risk markers" for harmful sexual behavior among college men (Wright et al., 2020, p. 4). "Men who have failed to develop empathy for others," and who hold hostile and antisocial views toward others makes them "predisposed toward violence and aggression" (Gray et al., 2017, p. 37). Psychopathy and narcissism are also associated with higher risk of engaging in harmful sexual behavior and include traits like "shallow and callous affect, egocentricity, lack of remorse and empathy for others and a tendency to manipulate others" (Grey et al., 2017, p. 37). Narcissism includes similar personality traits, including a strong emphasis on lack of empathy for others. Overall, these traits contribute to a higher likelihood of harmful sexual behavior because they "facilitate hostility toward women and anger when their perceived entitlement to sex is threatened" (Gray et al., 2017, p. 37).

Patterns of harmful behavior differ depending on whether someone engages in one-time or repeat harmful sexual behaviors. Generally, men who repeat harmful sexual behaviors possess more individual level factors, including traits associated with psychopathy and narcissism than men who engage in opportunistic, one-time harmful sexual behavior. Additionally, men who engage in one-time or repetitive harmful sexual behaviors differ on the level of remorse and guilt they express. Men who engage in repeated harmful sexual behavior express less remorse and guilt than men who engage one time. Men who engage in one-time harmful sexual behavior expressed that they learned something from being called out on their behavior (Abbey et al., 2012).

Clearly, different patterns of harmful sexual behavior call for different kinds of intervention. If men who engage in repeated harmful sexual behavior express less remorse and display more individual level traits associated with psychopathy and narcissism, interventions for them must begin long before college and focus on developing empathy and appropriate attachment in interpersonal relationships. Similarly, if men who engage in harmful sexual behavior only once express remorse and that they can learn from their bad behavior, it stands to reason that some interventions could address men who have or may engage in harmful sexual behavior by intervening with men who have or may cause harm. Specifically, these interventions should approach these men as people who may engage in harmful sexual behavior, rather than innocent bystanders. Educational programs should focus on what constitutes sexual violence and how their socialization into stereotypical gender roles (i.e., hyper-masculinity) may lead them to interpret women's resistance to their sexual advances as playful or something to be overcome, rather than actual nonconsent to sexual activity (Abbey & Jacques-Tiura, 2011; Loh et al., 2005).

Finally, addressing men who have or may engage in harmful sexual behavior requires significant attention to nuance and complexity. Given that men who engage in sexual violence use a variety of strategies and tactics to harm people, intervening with them requires a number of strategies. Unfortunately, given the complex ways gender socialization and power work in most western cultures, some people who engage in sexual violence may not even know what they are doing is harming another person. People who engage in harmful sexual behavior unquestionably use sex as a tool to exert their power over other people, yet some people who cause harm are unaware that their behaviors are rooted in power and entitlement – they have been socialized to believe that they have the right to control other people through physical, emotional, and mental coercion, as explored more in Chapter 2. Clearly, intervening with people who have been socialized to unconsciously exert their power over others through coercion requires deep, complex interventions implemented over time and in a variety of settings.

CONCLUSION

Educating students about sexual violence is complex and requires time and creativity. Unfortunately, most educational programs implemented and evaluated on college campuses over the past three decades show little change in terms of prevalence of sexual violence (Kettrey et al., 2023; Muehlenhard et al., 2017). Although the programs may show changes in students' rape myth acceptance or attitudes toward rape immediately after the program (Anderson & Whiston, 2005; Kettrey et al., 2023), those changes may or may not result in an actual change in behavior. Certainly, one of the greatest challenges educators and administrators manage around sexual violence education is evaluation of programs. It is nearly impossible to connect one-time educational programs with changes in behavior, especially sexually violent behavior. Further, given the resources educators and administrators have, evaluation of the programs falls to the bottom of the priority list. Instead, administrators simply focus on meeting the federal mandate that they provide education or training. Although educating the entire campus community about sexual violence is an important piece of preventing sexual violence, primary prevention programs – those aimed at stopping harmful sexual behavior before it starts – warrant increased attention on college and university campuses (ACHA, 2008).

Potentially the most crucial aspect of a comprehensive sexual violence program on college campuses, primary prevention efforts typically receive the fewest resources and are frequently conflated with response to sexual violence. To eradicate sexual violence on college campuses, educators and administrators must intervene with people who have or may engage in harmful sexual behaviors to stop sexual violence before it happens. As uncomfortable and challenging as it might be to identify people who may cause harm, knowledge and information are available. Administrators and educators rarely avoid profiling people who are at high risk for being targeted for sexual violence and must not shy away from identifying people who are at high risk for causing sexual violence either. Although administrators and educators have been working to educate college students about sexual violence for decades, the prevalence of sexual violence on college campuses has not budged (Muehlenhard et al., 2017). In the next chapter, I turn to examining strategies for more effective awareness, prevention, and response to sexual violence among college students.

6

STRATEGIES FOR EFFECTIVELY ADDRESSING SEXUAL VIOLENCE THROUGH A POWER-CONSCIOUS LENS

ABSTRACT

In this chapter, I reintroduce the power-conscious framework and the awareness–response–prevention trifecta undergirding this book. I summarize the previous chapters, including critiques of best practices related to addressing sexual violence among college students. I then highlight specific strategies for engaging in more effective awareness, response, and prevention of sexual violence among college students.

Keywords: Strategies; sexual violence; response; awareness; prevention

Throughout this book, I have examined history and current practices related to addressing sexual violence on college campuses. Using a power-conscious framework, I critiqued current practices and challenged educators and administrators to consider the historical foundations of sexual violence and awareness, response, and prevention of sexual violence. In this chapter, I provide some ideas to consider as we move forward in addressing sexual violence on college and university campuses. Some of these ideas, or an iteration of them, may already be taking place in some spaces. Unfortunately, critical, transformative work is sometimes buried in the deep corners of college and university campuses because it does not align with a well-known "best practice" and is often being done by people working quietly in the margins of our institutions. Many times, these radical educators are intentionally trying not to be discovered for fear of being reprimanded, asked to stop doing what they're doing, or co-opted by mainstream sexual violence organizations. My hope is that by putting forth ideas in a published manner that they may become seen as "best practices" and some educators will feel supported in voicing what they have known to be true for a very long time. Maybe with this support, more critically minded people can do the work that is so crucial for effectively addressing sexual violence through a power-conscious lens, rather than being shut-down through cautionary compliance-focused responses to sexual violence.

In this chapter, I revisit the power-conscious framework and awareness–response–prevention trifecta outlined in Chapter 1 for addressing sexual violence among college students. Specifically, I highlight strategies for educators and administrators who want to be more mindful in addressing power in their practices related to sexual violence. Finally, I end the chapter with a call for administrators and educators to address sexual violence as a problem of equity rooted in oppression and dominance.

A CAUTION ON "INCLUSIVE" PRACTICES

Although many people advocate for the development of "inclusive" programs on college and university campuses, I caution against using this language. Not all programs or policies can be applicable to all people because power influences the ways in which people experience the same situation differently. Striving for "inclusive" programs or policies runs dangerously close to engaging in color-evasive ideologies, which ignore or minimize difference (Annamma et al., 2017). Attempting to create "inclusive" programs or policies stems from an assumption that one approach can work for everyone. Rather than aim toward inclusive policies or programs, I advocate that we work toward equitable policies and programs. Equitable programs require people to consider the ways people may experience a situation differently based on their identities and relationship to power and to explicitly address those differences in their work.

Inclusion practices are often power-neutral rather than power-conscious. For example, an "inclusive" approach to sexual violence education requires that educators use gender-neutral or vague language to refer to people who cause harm and people targeted for harm. The point of this is to ensure that it is clear that anyone can cause harm and anyone can experience harm. However, an equitable program would be one in which educators name that people who engage in harmful sexual behavior are men 98% of the time, regardless of the gender of the person being targeted (Black et al., 2011). Similarly, because the dominant narrative about sexual violence focuses on cisgender heterosexual white women, educators must also take every opportunity to note that people who cause harm target those with minoritized identities at even higher rates than cisgender heterosexual white women (Cantor et al., 2019). Failing to name the reality that sexual violence is directly related to dominance and oppression perpetuates the invisibility of people who cause harm, resulting in educational programs where those targeted for sexual violence are expected to end violence. Power-neutral approaches reify dominant narratives; power-conscious approaches interrupt dominant narratives, providing nuance to the ways that people understand sexual violence.

POWER-CONSCIOUS FRAMEWORK

Power-consciousness requires educators to employ a complex, nuanced approach to addressing students' needs. It necessitates that educators listen to and consider ways students' experiences and needs are different from each other in a variety of ways. As highlighted in Chapter 1, the power-conscious framework guiding this text rests on three assumptions: (a) engage in critical consciousness and self-awareness; (b) consider history and context when examining issues of oppression; (c) change behaviors based on reflection and awareness; (d) name and interrogate the role of power in individual and systemic practices; (e) divest from privilege; and (f) work in solidarity to address oppression. A power-conscious framework (see Fig. 1) supports educators and administrators in thinking about ways to develop more equitable and effective approaches to addressing sexual violence.

Similarly, awareness, response, and prevention are all important components of addressing sexual violence on college campuses. As highlighted throughout the text, these three components often get conflated as *prevention* in sexual violence work on college campuses. In this text, I attempted to

Strategies for Effectively Addressing Sexual Violence 135

POWER-CONSCIOUS FRAMEWORK

- Engage in critical consciousness and self-awareness
- Consider history and context
- Change behaviors based on reflection and awareness
- Name & interrogate the role of power in individual & systemic practices
- Divest from privilege
- Work in solidarity to eradicate oppression

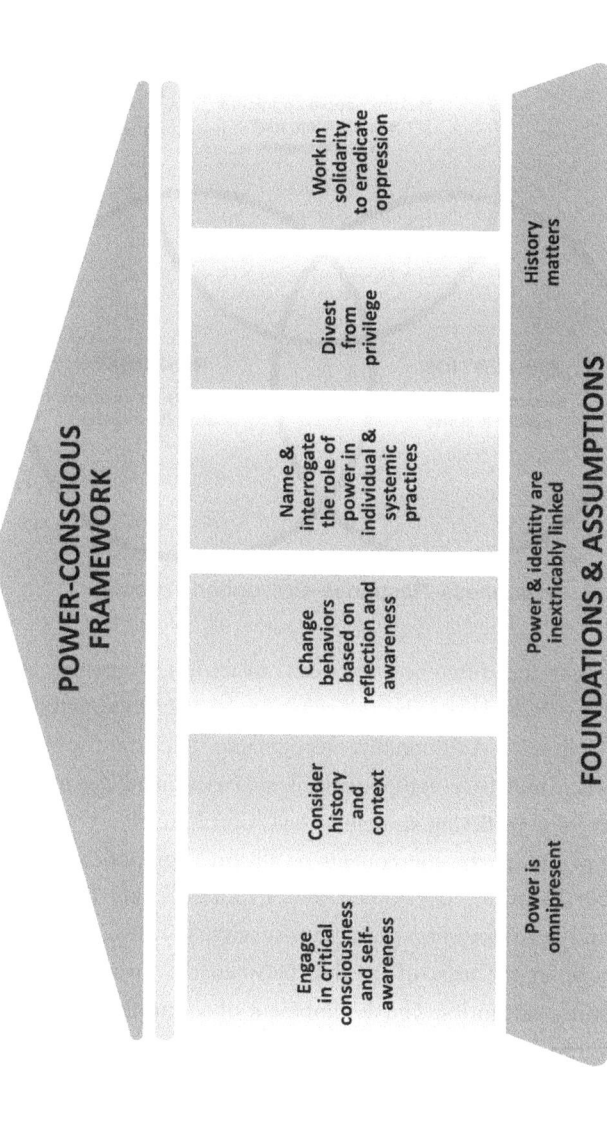

FOUNDATIONS & ASSUMPTIONS

- Power is omnipresent
- Power & identity are inextricably linked
- History matters

Fig. 1. Power-Conscious Framework.

AWARENESS
Making people cognizant of a problem and its significance

PREVENTION
Stopping violence before it starts

RESPONSE
Addressing violence after it happens

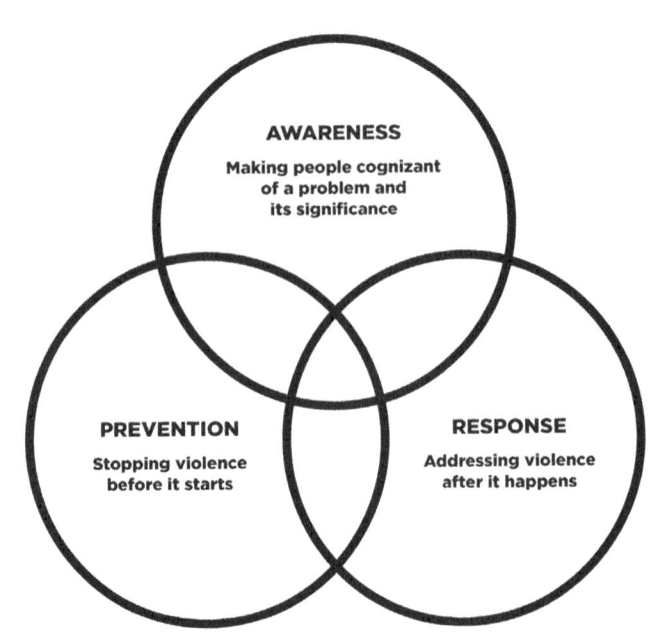

Fig. 2. Awareness–Response–Prevention Trifecta.

highlight the differences between awareness, response, and prevention and describe the significance of each component (see Fig. 2). Additionally, recognizing important overlap between the three components, I also examined the importance of considering strategies that contribute to a combination of two of the components or all three components.

For example, developing and making people aware of culturally competent resources for survivors of sexual violence may fit in the area of overlap between the awareness and response categories. The development of culturally competent resources is an example of response and making people aware of the resources is an example of awareness. Similarly, intervening with people who cause harm is an example of the overlap between response and prevention. Although intervening with people who cause harm is not a form of *primary* prevention (i.e., stopping violence before it happens), it is an example of stopping violence from happening again. Therefore, intervening with people who cause harm is both a form of response and prevention.

Recognizing the synergy between awareness, response, and prevention is important in moving forward to address campus sexual violence. Although I separate awareness, response, and prevention into three distinct chapters, I do not mean to imply that they cannot exist together. In fact, although different administrators and educators on campuses may be responsible for different aspects of addressing sexual violence, these efforts should be coordinated and educators and administrators must work together to ensure that the efforts complement each other, rather than detract from or contradict each other. For example, while primary prevention (i.e., working with people who have or may cause harm) should not take place in the same space as services for survivors of sexual violence, it is important for the people coordinating primary prevention programs and services for survivors communicate with each other to ensure that both groups are aware of the trends and issues that they are both seeing. Communication with each other allows educators to stay aware of emerging patterns and trends, resulting in more effective prevention and response.

Similar to the ways in which I divided the book into three chapters focusing on awareness, response, and prevention even though the three areas have overlap, I do the same in making recommendations for developing power-conscious approaches to addressing sexual violence among college students.

AWARENESS

As outlined in the chapter on awareness of sexual violence, an important component of addressing sexual violence on college campuses is to help people understand the significance and complexity of the problem of sexual violence. Additionally, making people aware of resources available for education and response to sexual violence is an important component of awareness.

One of the challenges discussed in Chapter 3 included making students aware of the complexity of sexual violence. Many students are aware of the scope of the problem of sexual violence. Thanks to media (including campus newspapers), student activists, social media, and personal experiences, many students know that sexual violence affects an alarming number of their peers (Cantor et al., 2019; McMahon & Stepleton, 2018). However, students also tend to have a misconception of how sexual violence happens and who typical victims of sexual violence are. For example, when asked to describe their strategies for safety on campus, many students describe tactics consistent with protecting themselves from stranger assault like never walking alone at night, carrying weapons, and talking on their phones as they walk around campus at night (Linder & Lacy, 2019).

Similarly, because sexual violence covers a wide variety of behaviors, students may also be confused about what constitutes sexual violence. To add further confusion, language used in research, legal processes, and education are inconsistent. For example, researchers use the words *unwanted sexual touching, sexual coercion, incapacitated rape, forcible rape,* and *sexual assault.* Campus adjudication programs often use the terms *sexual misconduct* and *nonconsensual sex* (deHeer & Jones, 2017; Linder, Richards, et al., 2024; Wood et al., 2017). Further, educators typically talk about *sexual assault* or *sexual violence* more broadly, and sometimes focus exclusively on illegal, rather than harmful, behaviors (Linder, Richards, et al., 2024). Given that each of these terms mean different things in different contexts, educating students about the nuances and dynamics of sexual violence becomes incredibly challenging.

Further, because many media outlets and scholarship portray targets of sexual violence as white, cisgender, heterosexual women, and people who cause harm as strangers and men of color, students also likely have misperceptions about the people involved in sexual violence. Misperceptions about targets for sexual violence and people who cause sexual harm result in students failing to intervene in potential bystander situations (examined in the "prevention" section of this chapter), and some survivors not considering their experiences legitimate, resulting in them not seeking support in the aftermath of sexual violence (Ameral et al., 2020; Karunaratne, 2023). To address these challenges, campus educators and administrators may consider several strategies for creating more power-conscious awareness-raising tools.

Invest time and resources. Educators and administrators must invest the time and resources necessary to educate students about sexual violence and consider a number of factors on their campuses. For example, campus leaders frequently require students to participate in a session at orientation that covers several "problems" on campus: sexual assault, alcohol, and diversity. This is highly problematic for many reasons, including the conflation of alcohol and sexual assault, which presents an inaccurate picture of sexual assault being about alcohol rather than about power. Further, adding "diversity" to a session with alcohol and sexual violence presents "diversity" as a problem to be dealt with rather than an asset. These one-time programs often result in little to no information being retained (Newlands & O'Donohue, 2016) because students are so overwhelmed with the amount of information they receive at once.

Some campuses have moved from a one-time program at orientation to requiring students to complete an online training about alcohol and/or sexual violence prior to enrolling in classes (Newlands & O'Donohue, 2016). Online training modules are time-efficient and meet federal mandates for campus administrators to educate students about sexual violence. Unfortunately, students frequently do not retain this information either. Students report clicking through the training while they are engaged in a number of other activities, not paying attention to the material presented (Karunaratne & Harris, 2022; Smith, 2015). To more effectively educate students about sexual violence, administrators must create the time and opportunity for students to engage in on-going educational programming focused on the nuance and complexity of sexual violence, focusing specifically on various identity and affinity groups (Chugani et al., 2021; Wooten, 2017; Worthen & Wallace, 2017, 2021; Zounlome et al., 2019). As described the prevention section of this chapter, all community members must be invested in educating students about sexual violence.

Develop identity-specific educational workshops. Students benefit from identity-specific education related to sexual violence (Anderson & Whiston, 2005; Vladutiu et al., 2010; Worthen & Wallace, 2017). For example, queer and trans students may benefit from a workshop that specifically focuses on dynamics of sexual violence in LGBT communities. Similarly, students of color, who are frequently ignored in mainstream sexual violence education, may benefit from educational programs organized through multicultural student organizations or cultural centers on campus. Providing opportunities for students to engage with people who share similar experiences to them would allow for more in-depth opportunities to ask questions, engage, and better understand issues of sexual violence. However, administrators cannot expect the already overworked staffs in these offices to do this work without additional resources. Sexual violence prevention and education must be funded and supported through professional development in order to be effective.

Provide accurate information about the history, dynamics, and definitions of sexual violence. Although many college students arrive on campus fully prepared to ward off strangers and crime, it would behoove educators and administrators to take a "yes, and[…]" approach to addressing students' concerns around crime. While it is certainly important for students to remain mindful of reducing their risk of victimization from various crimes that may be committed by strangers, they should also be made aware of the actual dynamics of sexual violence. If students were more aware that sexual violence is most likely committed by someone known to the victim, rather than a stranger (Cantor et al., 2019), they may learn to take different precautions when around people who they have been socialized to uncritically trust. Although it is never a potential target's responsibility to stop violence from happening, some risk reduction strategies may result in fewer incidents of violence. Teaching students about the characteristics and patterns of harmful sexual behavior may contribute to an increased awareness of potential signs of more common instances of sexual violence, which may also contribute to risk reduction.

Given the complexities of definitions of sexual violence and consent, educators and administrators may also consider educational workshops focused on examining harmful behaviors rather than simply focusing on illegal ones. Creating spaces for students to explore harmful behaviors may decrease defensiveness and increase openness to considering ways they have engaged in harmful behaviors. People often become fearful when discussions related to legal issues arise because they do not want to "get in trouble." Focusing on harm, including ways that we all participate in harm, may reduce defensiveness and allow people to identify harmful behaviors that they may not have previously identified as harmful, and stop engaging in those behaviors.

Further, by defining consent and providing examples of what consent is and is not, students may have a better understanding of what constitutes sexual violence and consider changing their behavior accordingly. Similarly, because sexual violence is frequently portrayed as an issue connected to high-risk alcohol use, helping students understand the power dynamics present in sexual violence may contribute to a more accurate understanding of sexual violence, which may reduce people's likelihood causing or experiencing harm. Specifically, teaching people – faculty, staff, and students – the history of sexual violence as a tool of colonization, terrorization, and economic exploitation may result in them having a deeper understanding of the relationship between power and sexual violence. This deeper understanding may be both empowering for survivors (Harris, 2020) and contribute to a reduction in risk for potential targets.

One of the challenges associated with educating students accurately about sexual violence is the fear the public relations ramifications of discussing consent in climates where students (and in some cases their parents) are not comfortable discussing sexual activity or admitting that college students, in fact, engage in sexual activity. Further, by discussing sexual violence as early as orientation to college, some administrators express concern that they risk portraying their campuses as unsafe. To address this challenge, educators and administrators could present statistics about campuses nationally, acknowledging that sexual violence is a problem on every campus and that they are proactively working to address the problem, rather than waiting until after it happens.

RESPONSE

As discussed in Chapter 4, as a result of carceral federal policy, college and university administrators experience a considerable amount of pressure to spend resources responding to sexual violence after it happens, distracting from preventing it from happening in the first place. Specifically, most policy focusing on campus sexual violence requires campuses develop processes for adjudicating reports of sexual assault and for providing services to survivors of sexual violence in the aftermath of sexual violence (Duncan, 2014; Dunn, 2014; Tani, 2017). Unfortunately, thanks to overly complicated legislation, state and federal guidance, and confusion created by on-going lawsuits related to sexual violence on campus, many campus reporting systems are confusing to students (McMahon & Stepleton, 2018) and most also fail to consider the role of power and identity in adjudication processes (Collins, 2016). Many survivors report not wanting to participate in processes with only punitive options (Decker et al., 2022; Gartner et al., 2024; Ratajczak & Wingert, 2024), and punitive responses just perpetuate more violence (Kaba & Ritchie, 2022; Sered, 2019).

Interpretation of federal policies related to sexual violence also put confidential healing spaces for survivors at risk (Holland et al., 2018). Risk management-oriented interpretations of policies compel faculty and staff to report disclosures of sexual violence to campus authorities, with or without survivor consent. Referred to as "mandatory reporting," compelled disclosure policies are far from trauma-informed policies and students often experience mandatory reporting as a form of institutional betrayal (Gartner et al., 2024).

Finally, virtually no campuses provide appropriate services for people who engage in sexual violence. Given that many people who cause harm often do so as a result of their own experiences with trauma, intervention programs to educate and transform the behavior of people who cause harm require increased attention. Responding effectively and equitably to campus sexual violence is a significant piece of the puzzle when it comes to comprehensively addressing sexual violence and several strategies warrant attention from administrators and educators.

Consider compliance a floor, not a ceiling. Compliance culture has a negative impact on almost all aspects of addressing sexual violence among college students. Well-intended policymakers have contributed to over-complicating campus response to sexual assault by failing to engage in power-conscious, nuanced discussions on the complexity of sexual violence. Campus administrators end up spending more resources on complying with law than on engaging in thoughtful discussion about ways to more effectively address violence in their specific contexts (Collins, 2016; Silbaugh, 2015). To address this problem, educators, administrators, and activists must remember that complying with mandates is the minimum we need to engage in, not the maximum. For example, if interpretation of Title IX guidelines requires that we provide "services for respondents," we should engage in thoughtful discussion about what that looks like. Mental health professionals have been working with people who cause harm for many years and can provide insight for Title IX staff about how to compassionately engage with people who cause harm by both holding them accountable for their harmful behaviors and exploring what healing they need to avoid causing future harm (Henkle et al., 2020; Rapisarda et al., 2020; Wilgus & Tabachnick, 2020).

The Campus SaVE Act requires colleges and universities to provide education for students related to sexual violence and requires that the education include attention to risk reduction, bystander intervention, and education about resources (Collins, 2016). That said, the policy does not prohibit colleges and universities from going beyond these three requirements to provide more in-depth, nuanced education. However, the hyperfocus on complying with policies results in administrators and educators having little time to consider what they might do beyond what is required.

Distinguish between punishment and accountability. Survivors of sexual violence frequently tell us that punitive responses to violence do not meet their needs for healing and recovery from violence (Decker et al., 2022; Gartner et al., 2024; Ratajczak & Wingert, 2024). In fact, most survivors do not want the person who caused harm to "get in trouble"; rather, they want them to change their behavior. Because punitive responses are something done to a person who causes harm, rather than something they choose to engage with, they do not bring the survivor healing or justice. To heal from violence, survivors report that they need the person who caused harm to acknowledge the harm and rectify their behaviors (Sered, 2019).

Campus responses mimic the criminal punishment system largely because of compliance and risk management (Collins, 2016). As highlighted in Chapter 4, campus administrators have felt pressured to prove their commitment to eradicating violence by punishing "individuals accused of such offenses harshly and swiftly" (Collins, 2016, p. 367), despite the reality that many survivors desire nonpunitive responses to violence. Some campus administrators have begun to explore restorative justice as a response to sexual violence, and interpretations of Title IX guidance have varied on whether or not this is permissible (Koss et al., 2014). Although restorative justice is an option for exploring nonpunitive responses to violence, it must be implemented intentionally and with a great deal of nuance. Unfortunately, as with most things that become codified or part of formalized processes, restorative justice may be co-opted or incorrectly used. The root of restorative justice is that both parties consent to participation: the people who caused harm acknowledge the harm caused, and they work to rectify it in the ways that the person who experienced harm need. The hyper legal culture related to addressing sexual violence contributes to people who have engaged in violence not feeling as though they can admit any wrongdoing, which prohibits restorative justice from being effective. Additionally, if not implemented with care, restorative justice may also contribute to the individualistic nature of harm, ignoring both the impact of violence on the larger community and the role of the larger community in perpetuating violence.

Many community organizers have begun to rely more on transformative justice principles than restorative justice principles for engaging in accountability rather than punishment (Dixon & Piepzna-Samarasinha, 2020; Hayes & Kaba, 2023). Transformative justice highlights the role of community in addressing and ending harm and requires community involvement in supporting both survivors and the people who have caused harm. For example, family members and friends of a person who caused harm may work with them to educate them about their behavior and develop specific interventions to teach them to stop. They then remain engaged with them to ensure that they continue working through their issues with power and control. At the same time, members of the community surround and uphold the survivor of violence, providing opportunities for healing (Dixon & Piepzna-Samarasinha, 2020). Examples of community accountability exist in queer communities and in communities of color (Hayes & Kaba, 2023), primarily because members of these communities do not have the luxury of ousting a member of the community and because formal justice systems typically do not work in favor of minoritized communities. College and university campuses may be another community in which community accountability processes may be effective (McMahon et al., 2019) if we are willing to engage in deep, nuanced work to really understand the roots of violence, including the ways that trauma impacts people who cause harm.

Protect confidential healing spaces for survivors and rethink mandatory reporting. A hyperfocus on compliance and risk management has resulted in the loss of many confidential spaces for survivors of sexual violence (Holland et al., 2018; Larson, 2023). Historically, campus policy carved out space for people with specific training on sexual violence response to be confidential spaces for survivors, meaning that those employees did not have a duty to report disclosures of violence to campus authorities. As Title IX has been interpreted and re-interpreted, spaces for confidential disclosures have narrowed considerably. Even victim-survivor advocacy centers no longer have complete confidentiality privilege on some campuses; they must report some instances of violence without the consent of the survivor.

As campus leaders work toward providing trauma-informed support for survivors, they should seriously reconsider the trauma-related implications of mandatory reporting. Removing choice from survivors about when and how their experience is shared is far from trauma-informed (Holland et al., 2021). Balancing the institutional need to know about violence with a survivor's well-being can be challenging. Both to comply with federal policy, *and* to fulfill the ethical obligation to prevent future violence, it makes some sense that campus administrators seek to know violence that occurs on campus so that they can intervene and prevent it from happening again. That said, given that most cases reported through administrative processes do not end in effective resolution, nor prevent people from engaging in future harmful behavior, the use of mandatory reporting is questionable.

Rather than instituting mandatory reporting to administrative offices focused on compliance, what if faculty and staff were trained to refer students to confidential victim-advocacy support instead? One of the objectives of mandatory reporting is to ensure that survivors receive the support they need, which is far more likely in victim-survivor advocacy services than in administrative adjudication offices.

Additionally, some faculty and staff have specific expertise in supporting students around issues of sexual violence. Campus administrators could provide opportunities for those faculty and staff to receive additional training and support to understand the various reporting options for students and be granted confidentiality privileges. Many faculty, especially those teaching in health and safety-related disciplines, teach about sexual violence in their courses. Inevitably, students will disclose their previous experiences with sexual violence in those spaces, and technically, faculty are required to report those disclosures. The mandatory reporting expectation discourages faculty and staff from engaging in discussions about sexual violence with students, which limits students' education around these topics, ultimately increasing risk for both experiencing and causing harm. Similarly, given that people who cause harm target people with minoritized identities at higher rates than their peers, providing support and carve-outs for staff who work in identity-based centers also warrants attention. If queer and trans students do not feel comfortable visiting the victim-survivor advocacy center on campus because they are unsure if the staff there will understand their experience, yet they feel comfortable sharing with staff in the LGBT resource center, that should be honored. Allowing staff in LGBT resource centers, cultural centers, and disability centers to serve as confidential resources may contribute to students' healing from sexual violence. Adjusting expectations around confidential spaces and mandatory reporting requires significant trust in faculty and staff and requires policymakers and risk managers to advocate for more nuanced policy.

Develop respondent services programs. In the next section about strategies for prevention, I will explore the importance of developing programs for people who have or may engage in harmful behavior from a mental health perspective. In this section, I advocate for the development of respondent services programs. Respondents have been accused of engaging in sexual misconduct and may or may not be found responsible for harmful behavior through a formal process. Because sexual misconduct adjudication processes have become more legalistic in nature, it is common for respondents to immediately become defensive and focused on the technical and legal aspects of the adjudication process (Roskin-Frazee, 2023). Respondent services professionals could support respondents in better understanding the adjudication process, which may reduce their defensiveness, allowing them to carefully examine why they were named as a respondent. Additionally, because people who are named as respondents in sexual misconduct cases likely engaged in at least some harmful behavior, even if it did not rise to the level of a policy violation, it is important to engage respondents in reflection about their behavior so that they do not continue harming people. Respondent services professionals may be able to serve as a compassionate guide for a respondent, helping them to understand the process they are engaging in and consider what may have led them to being in this process, including their own experiences with harm and trauma. Respondent services professionals could then help the respondent get connected with mental health or other services that could help them work through their experiences to prevent future harm.

Some people resist respondent services as a response to sexual violence because it seems as though we are privileging people who have engaged in harmful behavior. Using a punitive lens to address sexual violence would lead to this conclusion; however, given that nonpunitive responses to violence have a higher likelihood of contributing to survivor healing and ending future violence, it is important to reconsider this perspective. Respondent services are different from survivor advocacy programs. Respondent services provide compassionate education and guidance for respondents, but do not advocate that they are not responsible for causing harm.

PREVENTION

Primary prevention focuses on intervening before violence starts to ensure that it never happens (ACHA, 2008). In this section, I advocate for several strategies to push campus administrators and educators to focus on primary prevention of sexual violence. To do this, educators and administrators must take bold, innovative steps that may make some people uncomfortable. As illustrated throughout history, when the culture shifts and people who have historically enjoyed unlimited access to power and comfort are held accountable for their actions, a backlash often ensues. To effectively address sexual violence on college campuses, administrators must be prepared to handle a backlash from people who are used to enjoying comfort and power because of their social identities. Effectively intervening with people who have or may cause harm requires a focus on people with access to power – both formal and informal – which is difficult work.

Separate prevention and response offices. As the attention to sexual violence on college campuses has increased, so too have the resources dedicated to addressing sexual violence. Unfortunately, prevention and response of sexual violence are frequently conflated, and prevention and response strategies are lumped together into one program or office. When prevention and response are housed in the same location and share staff and resources, the crisis of responding to survivors of sexual violence will take precedent over engaging in prevention work. In the aftermath of a sexual assault, services and support for the survivor, including counseling, medical, legal, and advocacy, should be the focus of a well-funded, comprehensive sexual violence response center or program. Without a doubt, college and universities have a responsibility to provide culturally competent, thorough, and accurate support to survivors of sexual violence. Additionally, colleges and universities have a responsibility to more effectively engage in prevention strategies to stop sexual violence from happening before it starts, which requires a different set of skills than supporting survivors.

To engage in prevention activities more effectively, campus administrators may consider separating prevention and response functions into two separate offices or programs. Given that staff in sexual violence response and advocacy offices report being overwhelmed with more cases than they can handle and getting more and more complex cases requiring a significant amount of time (Ullman & Townsend, 2007), they cannot also be tasked with providing thoughtful, innovative primary prevention programming. Additionally, the training and skills required for supporting survivors are different from training and skills required to intervene with those who have or may cause harm. Although the foundation is the same, response and prevention are different.

Further, given the high likelihood that people providing support services to survivors of sexual violence experience vicarious or secondary trauma, asking them to then work with people who have engaged in sexual violence may trigger or exacerbate the trauma they have experienced. Secondary and vicarious trauma describe the ways that people in support roles begin to take on or internalize other people's trauma if not given the appropriate supervision and support for working through the cases they hear (Lynch, 2022). Vicarious and secondary trauma affect many people in helping professions, including counselors, doctors, and advocates. Rather than adding additional work to the already full agendas of sexual violence advocates, campus administrators should support advocates in doing their own healing work related to the trauma they experience from their jobs and hire additional people to engage in prevention programs with people who have or may cause harm.

Develop and implement programs for people who have or may engage in harmful sexual behavior. Although educating students to consider the ways they can reduce their risk of sexual violence is important and should be continued and improved, programs focused specifically on people who have or may engaged in harmful sexual behavior should also be embraced. Although some survivors and survivor advocates advocate for the expulsion of people who cause harm to protect victims and future victims from the behavior, expelling a person who causes harm from campus may result in the person going to a different community and continuing to perpetrate sexual violence. Given that college and university campuses have resources to develop innovative programs and educate members of their community, we are uniquely positioned to facilitate intervention with people who have engaged in harmful behavior. Further research is necessary to fully understand the characteristics and patterns of people who engage in harmful sexual behavior in college, yet enough research exists to begin to develop intervention and education programs directed at changing the behavior of people who cause harm. Additionally, as explored in Chapter 2, because so many people who engage in harmful sexual behavior also carry some trauma related to violence they have experienced in their own lives, supporting people who have engaged in harmful sexual behavior in their own healing through mental health counseling also warrants attention.

The current legal climate makes it challenging for campus administrators to knowingly keep people who cause harm on their campuses. No campus administrator wants to be responsible for having a person known to cause harm continue to cause harm. As seen in the cases of Jerry Sandusky at Penn State and Larry Nassar at Michigan State, some people who have engaged in sexual violence should immediately be removed from the community. However, as illustrated in Chapters 2 and 4, research indicates that some people, especially young people, who cause harm may benefit from educational interventions and can learn and understand how to change their behaviors. For this reason, colleges and universities may consider developing intervention programs for those who cause harm, especially low-level harm like ignoring another person's boundaries in everyday interactions.

When colleges and universities dismiss people who cause harm, many of them will go on to other communities (even if not another campus community) and continue engaging in sexual violence. Given that most college and university mission statements include a focus contributing to the betterment of society through innovative, research-oriented practices, developing intervention programs for those who have caused harm may fit into this mission. Similarly, given that some survivors – especially those who are members of minoritized communities – are uninterested in participating in formal criminal punishment processes or campus adjudication processes, intervention programs for those who cause harm may be a more power-conscious approach to addressing sexual violence in minoritized communities.

I frequently advocate for the development of programs designed to intervene with people who have or may cause harm and am regularly asked how I would identify those people if they were not "convicted" or "proven" guilty. Although the current legal climate focuses heavily on identifying perpetrators as either "bad" or "good" or "guilty" or "not guilty," intervention programs may require more gray area than this. If people are engaging in behavior that makes someone uncomfortable enough to report it to a campus authority, it is likely that person could benefit from some education around consent, power, and sex, even if they are not found responsible through the code of conduct for sexual violence. A behavior can be harmful without being illegal. Further, research provides plenty of information about the characteristics that make someone at risk for engaging in harmful sexual behavior, as outlined in Chapter 4. Rather than focusing on people who have or may engage in harmful behavior as bad people who should be ousted from a community, educators could identify people at high-risk for engaging in harmful behavior and approach sexual violence as part of an overall curriculum designed to engage people as responsible, productive members of a community.

It is also highly likely that people engaged in supporting and mentoring students on campus have heard of behaviors that raise red flags for them, but they do not have places to refer these students for assistance in unlearning this behavior for fear of "getting in trouble." Because sexual violence is rooted in power and dominance, many people who cause harm are unclear that their behavior is causing harm to anyone else. In many cases, people who cause harm – especially those who identify as men – are developing and demonstrating their worth through exerting power over others as they have been socialized to do. As many men will explain when they are given the opportunity to, jockeying for power this way is exhausting and only benefits some men. Counselors and critically conscious staff who advise student groups may be in a unique position to identify and refer people who have or may cause harm to programs specifically designed to help them understand and more effectively navigate the role of power in their lives.

Although some educators advocate for approaching all-male groups as potential allies and bystanders, rather than using the "bad dog" approach (Laker & Davis, 2011, p. 64), I advocate for something in the middle. Treating people who are at high-risk of causing harm as potential allies is dangerous. Failing to challenge people who have or may cause harm about their assumptions and beliefs about power and approaching men's groups as if there are no people who have or may cause harm in the space is dangerous. It perpetuates the notion that "we're all good guys here" which then does not give permission for people to intervene when they do see something that may be considered harmful. Further, failing to acknowledge and educate people that people who have or may cause harm are present all over campus perpetuates myths about who people who cause harm are and are not. As stated before, when students do not have an accurate understanding of who causes harm, they may be at higher risk for experiencing violence because they are socialized to be fearful of the wrong people, namely strangers and men of color, rather than the "good (white) college boy" sitting next to them in their biology class. Therefore, I advocate that we approach groups of students by naming that there are people who have or may cause harm in the space, just as we name that there are survivors in the space, as a way for them to think differently about their peer groups and maybe help some people who have or may cause harm to think twice about their behaviors. By explaining sexual assault and consent with nuance, some people who have or may cause harm may begin to question the behaviors and consider getting help for changing their behaviors.

Focus on education over training. As explored in Chapter 4, education and training are two different things. Education focuses on learning, while training focuses on specific ways to address a situation. Learning requires deep engagement from participants, allowing them to make sense of ideas, concepts, and perspectives from their own experiences, rather than being told what or how to think (Kulbaga & Spencer, 2019). Leaders and educators at institutions of higher education have a responsibility to provide opportunities for education and learning for students. Although policy mandates require campus leaders to document that they have provided education to students, this is only the starting point, not the ending point.

Providing opportunities for learning for students requires the engagement of the entire campus, rather than isolating these responsibilities to just a few people. Many faculty could engage students in learning about sexual violence in their disciplines as sexual violence has implications for a number of different fields. However, faculty must be supported in doing this work – they must have time to engage in their own on-going personal and professional development and be supported in not having to report every single student who discloses an instance of violence to the Title IX office. Faculty can use examples related to sexual violence in their coursework and develop entire units of their courses around the dynamics of sexual violence. For example, an economics professor could dedicate a unit of a course to discussing the economic impact of sexual violence on our communities. Further, a psychology or sociology professor could use a sexual experiences questionnaire to teach about research scale development. A marketing professor could partner with a community organization focused on sexual violence to allow students to practice developing marketing materials for the organization. Students learn both marketing, *and* about the dynamics of violence.

Not only does the process of engaging students in discussions on sexual violence matter, but so does the content. For too long, we have relied on the same kinds of educational programming focused on rape myth acceptance, understanding consequences of violence, developing empathy for survivors, and supporting survivors of violence, rather than digging into harmful behavior. When I read journal articles, job descriptions, and social media posts promoting sexual violence prevention, I often question what makes the program focused on prevention. Over and over and over again, we call programs focused on survivors "prevention" programs. I am continually puzzled by this. If a survivor exists, *we failed at prevention*. This does not mean that focusing on response to violence is not important – it definitely is. Having programs that teach students how to effectively respond when friends disclose violence to them are vitally important, *and they are not prevention programs.* It's ok to call them what they are – education designed to help us more effectively respond after violence occurs, and then we must go a step further and focus on actual prevention in our programs.

We do not have effective prevention programs because to effectively address violence, we must examine our own complicity in harmful environments. We must talk about things that are uncomfortable – like the fact that we, and people we love, engage in harmful behavior. We must address and examine power and we must engage in nuanced conversations, rather than framing people who cause harm as those bad, terrible, evil people "out there."

Creating programs that focus on interrupting harm, rather than reducing risk, require us to compassionately identify harmful behaviors and to distinguish between harmful and illegal behaviors. Creating spaces for students to explore harmful behaviors, rather than simply illegal behaviors, may decrease defensiveness and increase openness to considering ways they have engaged in harmful behaviors. People often become fearful when discussions related to legal issues arise because they do not want to "get in trouble." Focusing on harm, including ways that we all participate in harm, may reduce defensiveness and allow people to identify harmful behaviors that they may not have previously identified as harmful and stop engaging in those behaviors.

On college campuses, we have created a number of programs that focus on teaching people how to communicate boundaries and consent yet have spent less time teaching people how to understand and read other people's boundaries. In addition to teaching people how to express their needs, we must also teach people how to accept other people's needs, especially if other people's needs are in conflict with what we want. Imagine a program where we talk with students about what it feels like to experience what is perceived as a rejection and explore that rejection as a form of someone else expressing their needs, which often have nothing to do with the person receiving the perceived rejection.

Designing educational programs with nuance is hard. We have few examples and have been socialized to fear talking with students in nuanced ways because it may "cause confusion" or be too sensitive. This is on us as educators – students tell us repeatedly that they are ready for these conversations. They are hungering for them – it is us, the educators – who are afraid of them.

CONCLUSION

Overall, the basic, underlying principle of more effectively addressing sexual violence requires educators and administrators to consider sexual violence an equity issue rooted in issues of dominance and oppression, rather than solely seeing it as a public health issue. The historical roots of sexual violence as a tool of domination, colonization, and economic control illuminate the ways sexual violence continues to thrive on college campuses today. By referring to campus sexual violence as a "national epidemic," researchers, journalists, and activists disassociate campus sexual violence from larger systems of dominance and oppression. Epidemic implies a "short-term, isolated problem" (Deer, 2015, p. ix) and does not take into account how sexual violence has remained a constant form of power and control throughout history. Although helping people – students, parents, faculty, staff, and policymakers, among others – understand the relationship between power and sexual violence is complicated, failing to do so is unethical. Rates of sexual violence on college campuses have not changed in over 60 years (Muehlenhard et al., 2017) meaning that current practices have not been effective. Further, given that people who cause harm target those in minoritized communities at higher rates than their dominant group peers (Cantor et al., 2019), considering sexual violence a manifestation of power, dominance, and oppression may not be so difficult to understand.

To more effectively address sexual violence, educators and administrators must embrace their courage: courage to speak truth to power, to try new and innovative approaches, to be bold and different, to take risks, and to embrace the complexity and nuance that challenging power has always required. To effectively eradicate sexual violence on campus and beyond, educators and administrators must listen to those in the margins of the margins, the people who know the effects of unchecked power and oppression better than anyone else. Continuing to center dominant groups in addressing sexual violence will not only cause harm to people in minoritized communities, but to everyone. Current strategies are not effective for anyone. What will it take for us to implement bolder, power-conscious approaches to addressing sexual violence on our campuses?

REFERENCES

Abbey, A., & Jacques-Tiura, A. J. (2011). Sexual assault perpetrators' tactics: Associations with the personal characteristics and aspects of the incident. *Journal of Interpersonal Violence*, 26(14), 2866–2889. https://doi.org/10.1177/0886260510390955

Abbey, A., Parkhill, M. R., Clinton-Sherrod, A. M., & Zawacki, T. (2007). A comparison of men who committed different types of sexual assault in a community sample. *Journal of Interpersonal Violence*, 22(12), 1567–1580. https://doi.org/10.1177/0886260507306489

Abbey, A., Wegner, R., Pierce, J., & Jacques-Tiura, A. J. (2012). Patterns of sexual aggression in a community sample of young men: Risk factors associated with persistence, desistance, and initiation over a one year interval. *Psychology of Violence*, 2(1), 1–15. https://doi.org/10.1037/a0026346

Ameral, V., Reed, K. M. P., & Hines, D. A. (2020). An analysis of help-seeking patterns among college student victims of sexual assault, dating violence, and stalking. *Journal of Interpersonal Violence*, 35(23–24), 5311–5335. https://doi.org/10.1177/0886260517721169

American College Health Association. (2008). Shifting the paradigm: Primary prevention of sexual violence. https://www.naspa.org/images/uploads/kcs/2008_ACHA_PSV_toolkit.pdf

Anderson, M. J. (2016). Campus sexual assault adjudication and resistance to reform. *The Yale Law Review, 125,* 1940–2005.

Anderson Wadley, B. L., & Hurtado, S. S. (2023). Using intersectionality to reimagine Title IX adjudication policy. *Journal of Women and Gender in Higher Education, 16*(1), 52–66.

Anderson, L. A., & Whiston, S. C. (2005). Sexual assault education programs: A meta-analytic examination of their effectiveness. *Psychology of Women Quarterly, 29*(4), 374–388. https://doi.org/10.1111/j.1471-6402.2005.00237.x

Annamma, S. A., Jackson, D. D., & Morrison, D. (2017). Conceptualizing color-evasiveness: Using dis/ability critical race theory to expand a color-blind racial ideology in education and society. *Race, Ethnicity and Education, 20*(2), 147–162. https://doi.org/10.1080/13613324.2016.1248837

Armato, M. (2013). Wolves in sheep's clothing: Men's enlightened sexism and hegemonic masculinity in academia. *Women's Studies: An Interdisciplinary Journal, 42*(5), 578–598. https://doi.org/10.1080/00497878.2013.794055

Bagagli, B. P., Chaves, T. V., & Fontana, M. G. Z. (2021). Trans women and public restrooms: The legal discourse and its violence. *Frontiers in Sociology, 6,* 1–14. https://doi.org/10.3389/fsoc.2021.652777

Bang, A., Kerrick, A., & Wuthrich, C. K. (2017). Examining bystander intervention in the wake of #BlackLivesMatter and #TransLivesMatter. In S. C. Wooten & R. W. Mitchell (Eds.), *Preventing sexual violence on campus: Challenging traditional approaches through program innovation* (pp. 63–85). Routledge.

Banyard, V. L., Moynihan, M. M., & Crossman, M. T. (2009). Reducing sexual violence on campus: The role of student leaders as empowered bystanders. *Journal of College Student Development, 50*(4), 466–457. https://doi.org/10.1353/csd.0.0083

Banyard, V. L., Plante, E. G., & Moynihan, M. M. (2004). Bystander education: Bringing a broader community perspective to sexual violence prevention. *Journal of Community Psychology, 32*(1), 61–79. https://doi.org/10.1002/jcop.10078

Bauer-Wolf, J. (2024, April 22). A look at 13 years of Title IX policy. *Higher Ed Dive.* https://www.highereddive.com/news/a-look-at-11-years-of-title-ix-policy/623810/

Baumgartner, F. R., & McAdon, S. (2017, May 11). There's been a big change in how the news media cover sexual assault. *Washington Post.* https://www.washingtonpost.com/news/monkey-cage/wp/2017/05/11/theres-been-a-big-change-in-how-the-news-media-cover-sexual-assault/?utm_term=.4af8c1dcc0cf

Bedera, N., & Nordmeyer, K. (2015). "Never go out alone": An analysis of college rape prevention tips. *Sexuality & Culture, 19,* 533–542. https://doi.org/10.1007/s12119-015-9274-5

Beeymn, G. (2022, August 22). College students are increasingly identifying beyond 'she' and 'he'. *The Conversation.* https://theconversation.com/college-students-are-increasingly-identifying-beyond-she-and-he-187338

Benjamin, R. (2019). *Race after technology: Abolitionist tools for the new Jim Crow.* Polity Press.

Bevacqua, M. (2000). *Rape on the public agenda: Feminism and the politics of sexual assault.* Northeastern University Press.

Black, M. C., Basile, K. C., Breiding, M. J., Smith, S. G., Walters, M. L., Merrick, M. T., Chen, J., & Stevens, M. R. (2011). *The National intimate partner and sexual violence survey*. National Center for Injury Prevention and Control, Centers for Disease Control and Prevention. https://www.nsvrc.org/publications/NISVS-2010-summary-report

Bohmer, C., & Parrot, A. (1993). *Sexual assault on campus: The problem and the solution*. Maxwell Macmillan.

Boje, D. M., & Rosile, G. A. (2001). Where's the power in empowerment? Answers from Follett and Clegg. *The Journal of Applied Behavioral Science*, 37(1), 90–117. https://doi.org/10.1177/0021886301371006

Boschert, S. (2022). *37 words: Title IX and fifty years of fighting sex discrimination*. The New Press.

Boyd, A., & McEwan, B. (2024). Viral paradox: The intersection of "me too" and #MeToo. *New Media & Society*, 26(6), 3454–3471. https://doi.org/10.1177/14614448221099187

Brecklin, L. R., & Forde, D. R. (2001). A meta-analysis of rape education programs. *Violence & Victims*, 16(3), 303–321.

Brenan, M. (2023, July 11). Americans' confidence in higher education down sharply. *Gallup*. https://news.gallup.com/poll/508352/americans-confidence-higher-education-down-sharply.aspx

Brown, A. M. (2020). *We will not cancel us and other dreams of transformative justice*. AK Press.

Brown, A. M. (2021). *Holding change: The way of emergent strategy facilitation and mediation*. AK Press.

Brownmiller, S. (1975). *Against our will: Men, women and rape*. Random House.

Bummiller, K. (2008). *In an abusive state: How neoliberalism appropriated the feminist movement against sexual violence*. Duke University Press.

Burke, F. (2021). *Unbound: My story of liberation and the birth of the Me Too movement*. Flatiron Books.

Burt, M. R. (1980). Cultural myths and supports for rape. *Journal of Personality and Social Psychology*, *38*(2), 217–230. https://doi.org/10.1037/0022-3514.38.2.217

Cantalupo, N. (2012). "Decriminalizing" campus institutional responses to peer sexual violence. *Journal of College and University Law*, *38*(3), 481–524.

Cantor, D., Fisher, B., Chibnall, S., Harps, S., Townsend, R., Thomas, G., Lee, H., Kranz, V., Herbison, R., & Madden, K. (2019). *Report on the AAU campus climate survey on sexual assault and misconduct*. Association of American Universities. https://www.aau.edu/issues/climate-survey-sexual-assault-and-sexual-misconduct

Chief Elk, L., & Devereaux, S. (2014, December 23). The failure of bystander intervention. *The New Inquiry*. https://thenewinquiry.com/failure-of-bystander-intervention/

Chugani, C. D., Anderson, J. C., Richter, R. K., Bonomi, A. E., DeGenna, N. M., Feinstein, Z., Jones, K. A., & Miller, E. (2021). Perceptions of college campus alcohol and sexual violence prevention among students with disabilities: "It was a joke". *Journal of Family Violence*, *36*(3), 281–291. https://doi.org/10.1007/s10896-020-00150-8

Clinton-Sherrod, M., Morgan-Lopez, A. A., Brown, J. M., McMillen, B. A., & Cowell, A. (2011). Incapacitated sexual violence involving alcohol among college women: The impact of a brief drinking intervention. *Violence Against Women*, *17*(1), 135–154. https://doi.org/10.1177/1077801210394272

Colburn, A., & Melander, L. A. (2018). Beyond Black and White: An analysis of newspaper representations of alleged criminal offenders based on race and ethnicity. *Journal of Contemporary Criminal Justice*, *34*(4), 383–398. https://doi.org/10.1177/1043986218787730

Collins, E. (2016). The criminalization of Title IX. *Ohio State Journal of Criminal Law*, *13*(2), 365–395.

Collins, P. H. (2000). *Black feminist thought: Knowledge, consciousness, and the politics of empowerment* (2nd ed.). Routledge.

Common Justice. (2020, May 4). The four guiding principles making our cities safer [video]. YouTube. https://www.youtube.com/watch?v=EQ3oyZ9w0fo&t=2s

Corrigan, R. (2013). *Up against a wall: Rape reform and the failure of success*. New York University Press.

Cottledge, A., Bethman, B., & Vlasnik, A. (2015). The academic feminist: We heart women's centers. http://feministing.com/2014/09/15/the-academic-feminist-we-heart-womens-centers/

Coulter, R. W. S., Maier, C., Miller, E., & Blosnich, J. R. (2017). Prevalence of past-year sexual assault victimization among undergraduate students: Exploring differences by and intersections of gender identity, sexual identity, and race/ethnicity. *Prevention Science*, *18*(6), 726–736. https://doi.org/10.1007/s11121-017-0762-8

Crenshaw, K. (1989). Demarginalizing the intersection of race and sex: A Black feminist critique of antidiscrimination doctrine, feminist theory, and anti-racist politics. *University of Chicago Legal Forum*, *1*, 139–167.

Crenshaw, K. W. (1991). Mapping the margins: Intersectionality, identity politics, and violence against women of color. *Stanford Law Review*, *43*(6), 1241–1299.

Cruz, J. (2021). The constraints and fear and neutrality in Title IX administrators' responses to sexual violence. *The Journal of Higher Education*, *92*(3), 363–384.

Culture of Respect. (2017). *The culture of respect CORE blueprint*. NASPA: Student Affairs Administrators in Higher Education.

Culture of Respect. (n.d.). Level of evidence. http://cultureofrespect.org/colleges-universities/programs/level-of-evidence/

Davis, A. Y. (2003). *Are prisons obsolete?* Seven Stories Press.

Decker, M. R., Holliday, C. N., Hameeduddin, Z., Shah, R., Miller, J., Dantzler, J., & Goodmark, L. (2022). Defining justice: Restorative and retributive justice goals among intimate partner violence survivors. *Journal of Interpersonal Violence*, *37*(5–6), NP2844–NP2867. https://doi.org/10.1177/0886260520943728

Deer, S. (2015). *The beginning and the end of rape: Confronting sexual violence in Native America*. University of Minnesota Press.

Deer, S. (2017). Bystander no more? Improving Federal response to sexual violence in Indian country. *Utah Law Review*, *2017*(4), 771–800.

deHeer, B., & Jones, L. (2017). Measuring sexual violence on campus: Climate surveys and vulnerable groups. *Journal of*

School Violence, 16(2), 207–221. https://doi.org/10.1080/ 15388220.2017.1284444

Delgado, R., & Stefancic, J. (2012). *Critical race theory: An introduction* (2nd ed.). New York University Press.

Dimock, M., & Wike, R. (2020, November 13). America is exceptional in the nature of its political divide. *Pew*. https:// www.pewresearch.org/short-reads/2020/11/13/america-is-exceptional-in-the-nature-of-its-political-divide/

Dixon, E., & Piepzna-Samarasinha, L. L. (2020). *Beyond survival: Strategies and stories from the transformative justice movement*. AK Press.

Donat, P. L., & D'Emilio, J. (1992). A feminist redefinition of rape and sexual assault: Historical foundations and change. *Journal of Social Issues*, 48(1), 9–22.

Duncan, S. H. (2014). The devil is in the details: Will the Campus SaVE Act provide more or less protection to victims of campus assaults? *Journal of College and University Law*, 40(3), 443–466.

Dunn, L. L. (2014). Addressing sexual violence in higher education: Ensurance compliance with the Clery Act, Title IX, and VAWA. *Georgetown Journal of Gender and the Law*, 15, 563–584.

Engle, J. C. (2015). Mandatory reporting of campus sexual assault and domestic violence: Moving to a victim-centric protocol that comports with federal law. *Temple Political & Civil Rights Law Review*, 42(2), 401–421.

Fisher, B. S., & Sloan, J. J., III (2003). Unraveling the fear of victimization among college women: Is the "shadow of sexual assault hypothesis" supported? *Justice Quarterly*, 20(3), 633–659.

Flannery, M. E. (2024, February 14). Anti-DEI laws take aim at students of color and LGBTQ+ students. *NEA Today*. https://www.nea.org/nea-today/all-news-articles/anti-dei-laws-take-aim-students-color-and-lgbtq-students#:~:text=Since%202023%2C%20state%20legislators%20have,of%20race%20or%20ethnicity%20in

Freedman, E. B. (2013). *Redefining rape: Sexual violence in the era of suffrage and segregation*. Harvard University Press.

Freire, P. (2000/1970). *Pedagogy of the oppressed* (30th anniversary ed.). Continuum.

Gámez-Guadix, M., Straus, M. A., & Hershberger, S. L. (2011). Childhood and adolescent victimization and perpetration of sexual coercion by male and female university students. *Deviant Behavior*, 32(8), 712–742. https://doi.org/10.1080/01639625.2010.514213

Gartner, R. E., Smith, E. K., Panichelli, M., & Ballard, A. J. (2024). Campus sexual violence and the cost of protecting institutions: Carceral systems and trans student experience. *Affilia: Feminist Inquiry in Social Work*. https://doi.org/10.1177/08861099241245951

Gersh, D. (1987). The corporate elite and the introduction of IQ testing in American public schools. In M. Schwartz (Ed.), *The structure of power in America: The corporate elite as a ruling class* (pp. 163–184). Holmes & Meier.

Giddings, P. (1984). *When and where I enter: The impact of Black women on race and sex in America*. HarperCollins Publishers.

Gidycz, C. A., Warkentin, J. B., Orchowski, L. M., & Edwards, K. M. (2011). College men's perceived likelihood to perpetrate sexual aggression. *Journal of Aggression,*

Maltreatment & Trauma, 20, 260–279. https://doi.org/10. 1080/10926771.2011.562480

Goodman, D. J. (2012). *Promoting diversity and social justice: Educating people from privileged groups*. Routledge.

Goodmark, L. (2021). Reimagining VAWA: Why criminalization is a failed policy and what a non-carceral VAWA could look like. *Violence Against Women*, 27(1), 84–101.

Goodmark, L. (2022). Assessing the impact of the Violence Against Women Act. *Annual Review of Criminology*, 5, 115–131.

Goodmark, L. (2023). *Imperfect victims: Criminalized survivors and the promise of abolitionist feminism*. University of California Press.

Gray, M. J., Hassija, C. M., & Steinmetz, S. E. (2017). Etiology of sexual assault perpetration. In *Sexual assault prevention on college campuses* (pp. 33–56). Routledge.

Greensite, G. (2009, November 1). History of the rape crisis movement. *California Coalition Against Sexual Assault*. http://www.calcasa.org/2009/11/history-of-the-rape-crisis-movement/

Grimes, N. (2022). Cyberviolence prevention & response: New considerations for higher education and student affairs. *Journal of Trauma Studies in Education*, 1(2), 33–42. https://doi.org/10.32674/jtse.v1i2.4834

Griner, S. B., Vamos, C. A., Thompson, E. L., Logan, R., Vázquez-Otero, C., & Daley, E. M. (2020). The intersection of gender identity and violence: Victimization experienced by transgender college students. *Journal of Interpersonal*

Violence, *35*(23–24), 5704–5725. https://doi.org/10.1177/ 0886260517723743

Hall, I. (2024, February 6). Self-care and Gen Z: How are young people protecting their mental health in 2024? *Pion!* https://www.wearepion.com/blog-posts/self-care-gen-z-mental-health

Harper, S. R. (2012). Race without racism: How higher education researchers minimize racist institutional norms. *The Review of Higher Education*, *36*(1), 9–29. https://doi.org/10.1353/rhe.2012.0047

Harris, J. C. (2017). Centering women of color in the discourse on sexual violence on college campuses. In J. C. Harris & C. Linder (Eds.), *Intersections of identity and sexual violence on campus: Centering minoritized students' experiences*. Stylus.

Harris, J. C. (2020). Women of color undergraduate students' experiences with campus sexual assault: An intersectional analysis. *The Review of Higher Education*, *44*(1), 1–30. https://doi.org/10.1353/rhe.2020.0033

Harris, J. C., Cobian, K. P., & Karunaratne, N. (2020). Reimagining the study of campus sexual assault. In L. Perna (Ed.), *Higher education: Handbook of theory and research* (Vol. 35, pp. 1–47). Springer.

Harris, J. C., Karunaratne, N., & Gutzwa, J. A. (2021). Effective modalities for healing from campus sexual assault: Centering the experiences of women of color undergraduate student survivors. *Harvard Educational Review*, *91*(2), 248–272.

Harris, J. C., & Patton, L. D. (2019). Un/Doing intersectionality through higher education research. *The Journal of Higher Education*, *90*(3), 347–372. https://doi.org/10.1080/00221546.2018.1536936

Hassan, S. (2022). *Saving our own lives: A liberatory practice of harm reduction*. Haymarket Books.

Hayes, K., & Kaba, M. (2023). *Let this radicalize you: Organizing and the revolution of reciprocal care*. Haymarket Books.

Hayes-Smith, R. M., & Levett, L. M. (2010). Student perceptions of sexual assault resources and prevalence of rape myth attitudes. *Feminist Criminology*, 5(4), 335–354. https://doi.org/10.1177/1557085110387581

Henkle, J. E., Dunlap, J., & Tabachnick, J. (2020). *Expanding the frame: Institutional responses to students accused of sexual misconduct*. NASPA Report.

Hersey, T. (2022). *Rest is resistance: A manifesto*. Little Brown Spark.

Hills, W., & Adams, B. (2023). You might be causing harm if...: A poster campaign from the McCluskey Center for Violence Prevention Research and Education. *Journal for Women and Gender Centers in Higher Education*, 1(1), 1–15.

Holland, K. J., Cortina, L. M., & Freyd, J. J. (2018). Compelled disclosure of college sexual assault. *American Psychologist*, 73(3), 256–268. http://doi.org/10.1037/amp0000186

Holland, K. J., Hutchison, E. Q., Ahrens, C. E., & Torres, M. G. (2021). Reporting is not supporting: Why mandatory supporting, not mandatory reporting, must guide university sexual misconduct policies. *PNAS*, 118(52), 1–4. https://doi.org/10.1073/pnas.2116515118

Hollander, J. A. (2014). Does self-defense training prevent sexual violence against women? *Violence Against Women*, 20(3), 252–269. https://doi.org/10.1177/1077801214526046

Hong, L. (2000). Toward a transformed approach to prevention: Breaking the link between masculinity and violence. *Journal of American College Health*, 48(6), 269–279. https://doi.org/10.1080/07448480009596268

hooks, b. (1994). *Teaching to transgress: Education as the practice of freedom*. Routledge.

Hosie, K. (2020, July 29). More than just Tok: Gen Z's activism on TikTok is outperforming the performative. *Reach3*. https://www.reach3insights.com/blog/tiktok-social-activism

Hudson-Fledge, M. D., Grover, H. M., Mee, M. H., Ramos, A. K., & Thompson, M. P. (2020). Empathy as a moderator of sexual violence perpetration risk factors among college men. *Journal of American College Health*, 68(2), 139–147.

Hurtado, A. (1996). *The color of privilege*. The University of Michigan Press.

Incite! Women of Color Against Violence. (2006). *Color of violence*. South End Press.

Johnson, A. G. (2006). *Power, privilege and difference* (2nd ed.). McGraw-Hill.

Kaba, M., & Ritchie, A. J. (2022). *No more police: A case for abolition*. The New Press.

Karunaratne, N. (2023). *Healing from campus dating violence: An intersectional analysis of narratives of women and femme students of color*. Unpublished doctoral dissertation.

Karunaratne, N., & Harris, J. C. (2022). Women of Color student survivors' perceptions of campus sexual assault prevention programming. *Violence Against Women*, 28(15–16), 3801–3824. https://doi.org/10.1177/10778012211070310

Katz, J., Merrillees, C., Hoxmeier, J. C., & Motisi, M. (2017). White female bystanders' responses to a Black woman at risk for incapacitated sexual assault. *Psychology of Women Quarterly*, *41*(2), 273–285. https://doi.org/10.1177/0361684316689367

Katz, J., & Moore, J. (2013). Bystander education training for campus sexual assault prevention: An initial meta-analysis. *Violence & Victims*, *28*(6), 1054–1067.

Kettrey, H. H., & Marx, R. A. (2019). The effects of bystander programs on the prevention of sexual assault across the college years: A systematic review and meta-analysis. *Journal of Youth and Adolescence*, *48*, 212–227. https://doi.org/10.1007/s10964-018-0927-1

Kettrey, H. H., Thompson, M. P., Marx, R. A., & Davis, A. J. (2023). Effectiveness of campus sexual assault prevention programs on attitudes and behaviors among American college students: A systematic review and meta-analysis. *Journal of Adolescent Health*, *72*, 831–844. https://doi.org/10.1016/j.jadohealth.2023.02.022

Kim, M. E. (2018). From carceral feminism to transformative justice: Women-of-color feminism and alternatives to incarceration. *Journal of Ethnic & Cultural Diversity in Social Work*, *27*(3), 219–233.

Kim, M. E. (2020). The carceral creep: Gender-based violence, race, and the expansion of the punitive state, 1973-1983. *Social Problems*, *67*, 251–269.

Klein, L. B., Brewer, N. Q., Mennicke, A., Christensen, M. C., Baldwin-White, A., Cloy, C., & Wood, L. (2021). Centering minoritized students in campus interpersonal violence research. *Journal of Family Violence*, *36*, 911–921. https://doi.org/10.1007/s10896-020-00223-8

Klein, L. B., Dawes, H. C., James, G., Hall, W. J., Rizo, C. F., Potter, S. J., Martin, S. L., & Macy, R. J. (2023). Sexual and relationship violence among LGBTQ+ college students: A scoping review. *Trauma, Violence, & Abuse*, 24(4), 219602209. https://doi.org/10.1177/15248380221089981

Knott, K. (2024, May 14). Political standoff over Title IX puts red state colleges in no-win situation. *Inside HigherEd*. https://www.insidehighered.com/news/government/2024/05/14/red-states-say-they-wont-comply-new-title-ix-rule#:~:text=Republican%20governors%20and%20other%20officials,have%20to%20follow%20the%20regulations

Koss, M. P. (1985, October). Date rape: The story of an epidemic and those who deny it. *Ms. Magazine*, 56.

Koss, M. P., Gidycz, C. A., & Wisniewski, N. (1987). The scope of rape: Incidence and prevalence of sexual aggression and victimization in a national sample of higher education students. *Journal of Counseling and Clinical Psychology*, 55(2), 162–170.

Koss, M. P., Wilgus, J. K., & Williamsen, K. M. (2014). Campus sexual misconduct: Restorative justice approaches to enhance compliance with Title IX guidance. *Trauma, Violence, & Abuse*, 15(3), 242–257. https://doi.org/10.1177/15248338014521500

Kulbaga, T. A., & Spencer, L. G. (2019). *Campuses of consent: Sexual and social justice in higher education*. University of Massachusetts Press.

Laker, J. A., & Davis, T. (2011). *Masculinities in higher education: Theoretical and practical considerations*. Routledge.

Larson, S. (2023). The feminist teacher's dilemma: Faculty labor and the culture of sexual violence in higher education. *Harvard Educational Review, 93*, 1–25.

Lawrence, H. Y., Fernandez, L., Lussos, R. G., Stabile, B., & Brockelman-Post, M. (2019). Communicating campus sexual assault: A mixed methods rhetorical analysis. *Technical Communication Quarterly, 28*(4), 299–316. https://doi.org/10.1080/10572252.2019.1621386

Lawyer, S., Resnick, H., Bakanic, V., Burkett, T., & Kilpatrick, D. (2010). Forcible, drug-facilitated, and incapacitated rape and sexual assault among undergraduate women. *Journal of American College Health, 58*(5), 453–460.

Levine, J., & Meiners, E. R. (2020). *The feminist and the sex offender: Confronting harm, ending state violence.* Verso Books.

Lindemann, B. S. (1984). "To ravish and carnally know": Rape in eighteenth-century Massachusetts. *Signs, 10*(1), 63–82.

Linder, C. (2018). *Sexual violence on campus: Power-conscious approaches to awareness, prevention, and response.* Emerald Publishing Limited.

Linder, C., Caradonna, C. Y., Hodges, Q., & Moore, A. (2024). Using epistemic injustice to examine the scholarship about sexual violence among minoritized students. *Violence Against Women.* https://doi.org/10.1177/10778012241247191

Linder, C., Grimes, N., Williams, B. M., Lacy, M. C., & Parker, B. (2020). What do we know about campus sexual violence? A content analysis of 10 years of research. *The Review of Higher Education, 43*(4), 1017–1040. https://doi.org/10.1353/rhe.2020.0029

Linder, C., & Johnson, R. (2015). Problematizing the role of men in sexual violence prevention movements. *Journal of Critical Thought and Praxis*, 4(1). https://doi.org/10.31274/jctp-180810-37

Linder, C., Karunaratne, N., & Grimes, N. (2024). *Thinking like an abolitionist to end sexual violence in higher education.* Routledge.

Linder, C., & Lacy, M. (2019). Blue lights and pepper spray: Cisgender college women's perceptions of campus safety and the 'stranger danger' myth. *Journal of Higher Education*. https://doi.org/10.1080/00221546.2019.1664195

Linder, C., Richards, J., Melton, H., Griffiths, A., Peters, C., & Lund, H. (2024). Words matter: How college students use and understand terms related to intimate partner, dating, and sexual violence. *Journal of College Student Development*, 65(1), 1–17. https://doi.org/10.1353/csd.2024.a919347

Loh, C. A., Gidycz, C. A., Lobo, T. R., & Luthra, R. (2005). Prospective analysis of sexual assault perpetration risk factors related to perpetrator characteristics. *Journal of Interpersonal Violence*, 20(10), 1325–1348. https://doi.org/10.1177/0886260505278528

Lund, E. M., & Thomas, K. B. (2015). Necessary but not sufficient: Sexual assault information on college and university websites. *Psychology of Women Quarterly*, 39(4), 530–538. https://doi.org/10.1177/0361684315598286

Lynch, R. J. (2022). The cost of professional helping in higher education. *New Directions for Student Services*, 177, 69–80. https://doi.org/10.1002/ss.20416

Malamuth, N. M. (1989). The attraction to sexual aggression scale, Part 1. *The Journal of Sex Research*, 26(1), 26–49.

Marine, S. B., & Hurtado, S. S. (2021). Association for the Study of Higher Education (ASHE) response to the Department of Education's May 2020 regulations on Title IX of the Higher Education Act of 1972. https://www.ashe.ws/Files/Position%20Taking/2021.03%20ASHE%20Response%20to%20ED%27s%20May%202020%20regulations%20on%20Title%20IX%20of%20the%20Higher%20Education%20Act%20of%201972.pdf

Martinéz-Aleman, A. M., & Marine, S. B. (2023). *Voices of campus sexual violence activists: #MeToo and beyond*. Johns Hopkins University Press.

McCummings, Z., Lingerfelt, N., & Young Americans, S. (2018, January 21). How student newspapers are tackling campus sexual assault. *Slate*. https://www.salon.com/2018/01/21/how-student-newspapers-are-tackling-campus-sexual-assault/

McGuire, D. L. (2010). *At the dark end of the street: Black women, rape, and resistance – A new history of the Civil Rights Movement from Rosa Parks to the rise of Black power*. Alfred A. Knopf.

McMahon, S. (2015). Call for research on bystander intervention to prevent sexual violence: The role of campus environments. *American Journal of Community Psychology*, 55(3–4), 472–489. https://doi.org/10.1007/s10464-015-9724-0

McMahon, S., Burnham, J., & Banyard, V. L. (2020). Bystander intervention as a prevention strategy for campus sexual violence: Perceptions of historically minoritized college students. *Prevention Science*, 21(6), 795–806. https://doi.org/10.1007/s11121-020-01134-2

McMahon, S., Postmus, J. L., & Koenick, R. A. (2011). Conceptualizing the engaging bystander approach to sexual violence prevention on college campuses. *Journal of College Student Development*, *52*(1), 115–130.

McMahon, S., & Stepleton, K. (2018). Undergraduate exposure to messages about campus sexual assault: Awareness of campus resources. *Journal of College Student Development*, *59*(1), 110–115. https://doi.org/10.1353/csd.2018.0008

McMahon, S. M., Karp, D. R., & Mulhern, H. (2019). Addressing individual and community needs in the aftermath of campus sexual misconduct: Restorative justice as a way forward in the re-entry process. *Journal of Sexual Aggression*, *25*(1), 49–59.

Menakem, R. (2017). *My grandmother's hands: Racialized trauma and the pathway to mending our hearts and bodies*. Central Recovery Press.

Mendes, K., Ringrose, J., & Keller, J. (2019). *Digital feminist activism: Girls and women fight back against rape culture*. Oxford University Press.

Méndez, X. (2020). Beyond Nassar: A transformative justice and decolonial feminist approach to campus sexual assault. *Frontiers: A Journal of Women Studies*, *41*(2), 82–104.

Meyers, M. (2004). African American women and violence: Gender, race, and class in the news. *Critical Studies in Media Communications*, *21*(2), 95–188.

Mezirow, J. (1981). A critical theory of adult learning and education. *Adult Education*, *32*(1), 3–24.

Mohler-Kuo, M., Dowdall, G. W., Koss, M. P., & Wechsler, H. (2004). Correlates of rape while intoxicated in a national sample of college women. *Journal of Studies on Alcohol*, 65(1), 37–45. https://doi.org/10.15288/jsa.2004.65.37

Moynihan, M. M., & Banyard, V. L. (2008). Community responsibility for preventing sexual violence: A pilot study with campus Greeks and intercollegiate athletes. *Journal of Prevention & Intervention in the Community*, 36(1–2), 23–38. https://doi.org/10.1080/10852350802022274

Muehlenhard, C. L., Peterson, Z. D., Humphreys, T. P., & Jozkowski, K. N. (2017). Evaluating the one-in-five statistic: Women's risk of sexual assault while in college. *The Journal of Sex Research*, 54(4–5), 549–576. https://doi.org/10.1080/00224499.2017.1295014

Murnen, S. K., Wright, C., & Kaluzny, G. (2002). If "boys will be boys," then girls will be victims? A meta-analytic review of the research that relates masculine ideology to sexual aggression. *Sex Roles*, 46, 359–375. https://doi.org/10.1023/A:1020488928736

National Center for Education Statistics. (2017). Enrollment in elementary, secondary, and degree-granting postsecondary institutions, by level and control of institution, enrollment level, and attendance status and sex of student: Selected years, fall 1990 through fall 2026. https://nces.ed.gov/programs/digest/d16/tables/dt16_105.20.asp?current=yes

National Sexual Violence Resource Center. (2019). Sexual violence and transgender/non-binary communities. https://www.nsvrc.org/sites/default/files/publications/2019-02/Transgender_infographic_508_0.pdf

Nellis, A. (2021). The color of justice: Racial and ethnic disparity in state prisons. *The Sentencing Project*. https://www.sentencingproject.org/app/uploads/2022/08/The-Color-of-Justice-Racial-and-Ethnic-Disparity-in-State-Prisons.pdf

Newlands, R., & O'Donohue, W. (2016). A critical review of sexual violence prevention on college campuses. *Acta Psychopathologica*, 2(2), 1–13.

Nicolazzo, Z. (2016). "Just go in looking good": The resilience, resistance, and kinship-building of trans* college students. *Journal of College Student Development*, 57(5), 538–556. https://doi.org/10.1353/csd.2016.0057

Nicolla, S., & Lazard, A. J. (2023). Social media communication about sexual violence may backfire: Online experiment with young men. *Journal of Health Communication*, 28(1), 28–31. https://doi.org/10.1080/10810730.2023.2174214

Nicolla, S., Lazard, A. J., Austin, L. L., Freelon, D., Reyes, H. L. M., & Moracco, K. E. (2023). TikToks lead to higher knowledge and perceived severity of sexual violence among adolescent men. *Journal of Youth and Adolescence*, 52, 2449–2463. https://doi.org/10.1007/s10964-023-01867-7

NO. (n.d.). The rape documentary. https://www.notherapedocumentary.com/home

Okun, T. (2021). White supremacy culture: Still here. https://www.whitesupremacyculture.info/

Omi, M., & Winant, H. (1994). *Racial formation in the United States: From the 1960s to the 1990s*. Routledge.

One in Four. (n.d.). *One in Four*.http://www.oneinfourusa.org/nationalorganization.php

Page, C., & Woodland, E. (2023). *Healing justice lineages: Dreaming at the crossroads of liberation, collective care, and safety*. North Atlantic Books.

Patton, L. D. (2016). Disrupting postsecondary prose: Toward a critical race theory of higher education. *Urban Education*, 51(3), 315–342.

Patton, T. O., & Snyder-Yuly, J. (2007). Any four Black men will do: Rape, race, and the ultimate scapegoat. *Journal of Black Studies*, 37(6), 859–895.

Pecoraro, A. (n.d.). A history of sexual assault awareness month. *NWA Center for Sexual Assault*. https://www.nwasexualassault.org/a-history-of-sexual-assault-awareness-month

Pelfrey, W. V., Keener, S., & Perkins, M. (2018). Examining the role of demographics in campus crime alerts: Implications and recommendations. *Race and Justice*, 8(3), 244–269. https://doi.org/10.1177/2153368716675475

Peretz, T. (2023). A male feminist walks into a bar, because it was set so low: The pedestal effect and the economy of gratitude in feminist space. *Sociology Compass*, 1–19. https://doi.org/10.1111/soc4.13151

Porter, J., & McQuiller Williams, L. (2011). Intimate violence among underrepresented groups on a college campus. *Journal of Interpersonal Violence*, 26(16), 3210–3224. https://doi.org/10.1177/0886260510393011

Potter, S. J., & Stapleton, J. G. (2012). Translating sexual assault prevention from a college campus to a United States military installation: Piloting the Know-Your-Power bystander social marketing campaign. *Journal of Interpersonal Violence*, 27(8), 1593–1621. https://doi.org/10.1177/0886260511425795

Prior, S., & deHeer, B. A. (2023). *Campus sexual violence: A state of institutionalized sexual terrorism*. Routledge Press.

Radical Copy Editor. (n.d.). *Racial Copy Editor*. https://radicalcopyeditor.com/

Raffo, S. (2022). *Liberated to the bone: Histories, bodies, futures*. AK Press.

Rapisarda, S. S., Shields, R. T., & Tabachnick, J. (2020). *A new perspective on college sexual misconduct: Effective interventions for students causing harm*. MASOC.

Ratajczak, K., & Wingert, A. C. (2024). "It's not like I wanted him kicked off the football team": Alternative approaches to justice and campus sexual assault. *Crime & Delinquency*. https://doi.org/10.177/00111287241248108

Reid, A., & Dundes, L. (2017). Bystander programs: Accommodating or derailing sexism? *Behavioral Sciences*, 7(65), 1–13. https://doi.org/10.3390/bs7040065

Reuters. (2019). Kidnapped children make headlines, but abduction is rare in U.S. https://www.reuters.com/article/idUSKCN1P52BJ/#:~:text=Hundreds%20of%20thousands%20of%20juveniles,been%20abducted%20by%20a%20stranger

Ritchie, A. (2017). *Invisible no more: Police violence against Black women and women of color*. Beacon Press.

Roskin-Frazee, A. (2020). Protections for marginalised women in university sexual violence policies. *International Journal for Crime, Justice and Social Democracy*, 9(1), 13–30. https://doi.org/10.5204/ijcjsd.v9i1.1451

Roskin-Frazee, A. (2023). "Terrifying and exhausting": Secondary victimization in Title IX proceedings at U.S. higher education institutions. *Feminist Criminology*, 18(2), 114–132. https://doi.org/10.1177/15570851221105853

Rosner, H. (2021, October 8). The long American history of "missing white woman syndrome". *The New Yorker*. https://www.newyorker.com/news/q-and-a/the-long-american-history-of-missing-white-woman-syndrome

Schuller, K. (2021). *The trouble with white women: A counterhistory of feminism*. Bold Type Books.

Sered, D. (2019). *Until we reckon: Violence, mass incarceration, and a road to repair*. The New Press.

Sherman, S. A. (2022). Policing the campus: Police communications and near-campus development cross Atlanta's university communities. *Planning Theory & Practice*, 23(3), 368–387. https://doi.org/10.1080/14649357.2022.2050281

Silbaugh, K. (2015). *Reactive to proactive: Title IX's unrealized capacity to prevent campus sexual assault* (Vol. 95, pp. 1049–1076). Boston University Law Review.

Smith, T. (2015, August 12). Curbing sexual assault becomes big business on campus. National Public Radio. https://www.npr.org/2015/08/12/430378518/curbing-sexual-assault-becomes-big-business-on-campus

Spencer, C. M., Rivas-Koehl, M., Astle, S., Toews, M. L., Anders, K. M., & McAllister, P. (2022). Risk markers for male perpetration of sexual assault on college campuses: A meta-analysis. *Trauma, Violence, & Abuse*. https://doi.org/10.1177/15248380221097437

Stanek, C., & Mattson, G. (2024). 'At least you're not neurotypical': Stigma, mental illness disclosure, and social capital among privileged college students. *Deviant Behavior*, 45(2), 247–266. https://doi.org/10.1080/01639625.2023.2244118

Swartout, K. M., Swartout, A. G., Brennan, C. L., & White, J. W. (2015). Trajectories of male sexual aggression from adolescence through college: A latent class growth analysis. *Aggressive Behavior*, *41*, 467–477.

Takaki, R. (2023). *A different mirror: A history of multicultural America*. Back Bay Books.

Tani, K. M. (2017). An administrative right to be free from sexual violence? Title IX enforcement in historical and institutional perspective. *Duke Law Journal*, *66*, 1847–1903.

Tatum, B. D. (2000). Complexity of identity. In M. Adams, W. Blumenfield, R. Castaneda, H. Hackman, M. Peters, & X. Zuniga (Eds.), *Readings for diversity and social justice* (pp. 9–14). Routledge.

Testa, M., VanZile-Tamsen, C., Livingston, J. A., & Buddie, A. M. (2006). The role of women's alcohol consumption in managing sexual intimacy and sexual safety motives. *Journal of Studies on Alcohol and Drugs*, *67*(5), 665–674. https://doi.org/10.15288/jsa.2006.67.665

Thompson-Miller, R., & Picca, L. H. (2017). "There were rapes!": Sexual assaults of African American women and children in Jim Crow. *Violence Against Women*, *23*(8), 934–950. https://doi.org/10.1177/1077801216654016

Travis, J., Western, B., & Redburn, S. (2014). *The growth of incarceration in the United States: Exploring causes and consequences*. National Academies Press.

UCSD Center. (2019). Measuring #MeToo: A national study on sexual harassment and assault. https://www.raliance.org/wp-content/uploads/2019/04/2019-MeToo-National-Sexual-Harassment-and-Assault-Report.pdf

Ullman, S. E., & Townsend, S. M. (2007). Barriers to working with sexual assault survivors: A qualitative study of rape crisis center workers. *Violence Against Women*, *13*(4), 412–443. https://doi.org/10.1177/1077801207299191

Untied, A. S., Orchowski, L. M., Mastroleo, N., & Gidycz, C. A. (2012). College students' social reactions to the victim in a hypothetical sexual assault scenario: The role of victim and perpetrator alcohol use. *Violence & Victims*, *27*(6), 957–972.

Vitale, A. S. (2017). *The end of policing*. Verso Books.

Vladutiu, C. J., Martin, S. L., & Macy, R. J. (2010). College or university-based sexual assault prevention programs: A review of program outcomes, characteristics, and recommendations. *Trauma, Violence, & Abuse*, *12*(2), 67–86. https://doi.org/10.1177/1524838010390708

Wallace, P. S., Miller, K., Myers, K., Ingram, C., & Civilus, T. (2024). Framed as (un)victims of sexual violence: An intersectional model. *Feminist Criminology*. https://doi.org/10.1177/15570851241227937

Warshaw, R. (1988). *I never called it rape: The Ms. Report on recognizing, fighting, and surviving date and acquaintance rape*. Harper & Row.

Wesley, J. K., Brown, E. R., & Phills, C. E. (2022). Words matter: A qualitative content analysis of campus crime alerts and considerations for best practices. *Journal of American College Health*, *70*(1), 49–57. https://doi.org/10.1080/07448481.2020.1719114

West, L. M., Donovan, R. A., & Daniel, A. R. (2016). The price of strength: Black college women's perspectives on the Strong Black Woman stereotype. *Women & Therapy*, *39*(3–4), 390–412. http://doi.org/10.1080/02703149.2016.1116871

Whynacht, A. (2021). *Insurgent love: Abolition and domestic homicide*. Fernwood Publishing.

Wilgus, J. K., & Lowery, J. W. (2018). Adjudicating student sexual misconduct: Parameters, pitfalls, and promising practices. In J. Jessup-Anger & K. Edwards (Eds.), *Addressing sexual violence in higher education and student affairs* (pp. 83–94). New Directions for Student Services, no. 161. Jossey-Bass.

Wilgus, J. K., & Tabachnick, J. (2020). Incorporating what is known about respondents and their perspectives into thoughtful adjudication practices. In C. M. Renzetti & D. R. Follingstad (Eds.), *Adjudicating campus sexual misconduct and assault* (pp. 159–182). Cognella.

Willis, G. M. (2018). Why call someone by what we don't want them to be? The ethics of labeling in forensic/correctional psychology. *Psychology, Crime and Law*, 24(7), 727–743.

Wood, L., Sulley, C., Kammer-Kerwick, M., Follingstad, D., & Busch-Armendariz, N. (2017). Climate surveys: An inventory of understanding sexual assault and other crimes of interpersonal violence at institutions of higher education. *Violence Against Women*, 23(10), 1249–1267. https://doi.org/10.1177/1077801216657897

Wooten, S. C. (2017). Revealing a hidden curriculum of Black women's erasure in sexual violence prevention policy. *Gender and Education*, 29(3), 405–417. http://doi.org/10.1080/09540253.2016.1225012

Worthen, M. G. F., & Wallace, S. A. (2017). Intersectionality and perceptions about sexual assault education and reporting on college campuses. *Family Relations*, 66, 180–196. https://doi.org/10.1111/fare.12240

Worthen, M. G. F., & Wallace, S. A. (2021). "Why should I, the one who was raped, be forced to take training in what sexual assault is?" Sexual assault survivors and those who know survivors' responses to a campus sexual assault education program. *Journal of Interpersonal Violence*, 36(5–6), NP2640–NP2674. https://doi.org/10.1177/0886260518768571

Wright, L. A., Zounlome, N. O. O., & Whiston, S. C. (2020). The effectiveness of male-targeted sexual assault prevention programs: A meta-analysis. *Trauma, Violence, & Abuse*, 21(5), 859–869. https://doi.org/10.1177/1524838018801330

Zinzow, H. M., & Thompson, M. (2015). A longitudinal study of risk factors for repeated sexual coercion and assault in U.S. college men. *Archives of Sexual Behavior*, 44, 213–222. https://doi.org/10.1007/s10508-013-0243-5

Zounlome, N. O. O., Wong, Y. J., David, J., Klann, E. M., & Stephens, N. (2019). 'No one comes to save the Black girls…': Black university women's understanding of sexual violence. *The Counseling Psychologist*, 47, 873–908. https://doi.org/10.1177/0011000019893654

Zounlome, N. O. O., Wong, Y. J., Klann, E. M., & David, J. L. (2021). "I'm seen as a sexual predator from saying hello": Black men's perception of sexual violence. *Journal of Interpersonal Violence*, 36(19–20), NP10809–NP10830. https://doi.org/10.1177/0886260519877942

Printed and bound by CPI Group (UK) Ltd, Croydon, CR0 4YY
01/12/2024
14602894-0001